THE ORIGINS OF THE
MODERN EUROPEAN STATE
1450–1725

THE ORIGINS OF THE MODERN EUROPEAN STATE

1450–1725

J. H. Shennan
Reader in History, University of Lancaster

HUTCHINSON UNIVERSITY LIBRARY
LONDON

HUTCHINSON & CO (*Publishers*) **LTD**
3 *Fitzroy Square, London W*1

London Melbourne Sydney Auckland
Wellington Johannesburg Cape Town
and agencies throughout the world

First published 1974
© J. H. Shennan 1974

This book has been set in Monotype Bembo
Printed in Great Britain on smooth wove paper by
R. J. Acford Ltd., Industrial Estate, Chichester, Sussex,
and bound by Wm. Brendon, Tiptree, Essex

ISBN 0 09 119030 4 (cased)

0 09 119031 2 (paper)

CONTENTS

PREFACE

This book has taken shape in the course of twelve years of teaching the history of early modern Europe and my first debt therefore is to those twelve generations of undergraduates at the universities of Liverpool and Lancaster whose contributions have helped me to formulate my own ideas. I am also grateful to two friends and colleagues at Lancaster, Dr Martin Blinkhorn and Dr John Gooch, who encouraged me to write this book and in particular to my wife for her constant, often crucial advice and criticism. The imperfections of the final version remain, of course, my own responsibility.

Lancaster   J.H.S.

INTRODUCTION

The idea of the state as an abstract entity, representing neither government nor governed nor an alliance of both, is a familiar one to twentieth-century man. It was not always so, of course, and the manner in which it gradually impressed itself upon the European mind is a theme of great complexity. The object of this volume is to examine one particular phase of that process, beginning in the fifteenth century when personal, princely authority was becoming the chief source of political power in Europe and concluding early in the eighteenth century by which time the prince's power was ceasing to be indistinguishable from that of his kingdom and the concept of the impersonal state as the object of universal service and respect, from both rulers and ruled, was about to be crystallized. The following stage, the emergence of national states, lies outside the range of this volume.

Such a theme cannot be pursued in the context of a single country for it is only by comparing and contrasting developments in a variety of states that any common pattern may be discerned. Thus Russia as well as France and Spain, Denmark and Sweden as well as England, Italy as well as the United Provinces must be the subject of examination. Differences in social and political structure inevitably distort the time-scale and render the correlation between these countries imprecise. However, a model can be constructed which takes into account the wide-ranging variety between Russia at one end of the spectrum and Spain at the other. The historian's essential task, after all, is to impose a degree of order upon his subject, yet without fossilizing it altogether; though he must be especially on his guard against espying a spurious symmetry in so inchoate an area of study where the scale and scope are wide and the quarry particularly elusive.

In a recent collection of essays on Louis XIV's kingship one of the contributors has observed that 'the formation of the elements of the modern nation-state in the early modern period has not been much studied. The relationship of the dynastic monarchs . . . to the nation — however defined — is still less studied or understood'.[1] This remark implies a direct link between the state-structure of renaissance Europe and that of the present day which we may legitimately question, if only because it has not yet been demonstrated that the role of the community *vis-à-vis* the government was ever a crucial factor before the second half of the eighteenth century. Community consciousness, or proto-nationalism, has been emphasized on occasion as a vital element in the emergence of the modern state, but the opposite point of view, that government policies and decisions encouraged the growth of such a feeling, offers, as we shall see, a position at least as readily defensible.

However, the above quotation also recalls the significant fact that historians have not yet concerned themselves overmuch with an area which they are usually content to leave to the political theorist. The chief justification of this book, therefore, lies in the belief that so complicated a subject ought not to be studied solely in terms of political theory or linguistics; that to be fully appreciated and understood it requires an historian's orchestration. In discussing this very subject the Spanish historian, J. A. Maravall, has remarked that 'the Modern State is not a matter of theory alone: there is the practice as well'.[2] What follows, then, is an attempt to distinguish theory from practice without separating the one altogether from the other. Aided by the vision of political philosophers and the insights of practical politicians (sometimes though rarely, as with Thomas More, united in the same person) one can hope to discern how conclusions of universal validity may be drawn by a few acute and perceptive witnesses of changes in the political order, conclusions which in their turn make up an intrinsic part of succeeding mutations. It follows from this two-level approach that though the evolutionary nature of the theme requires a basically chronological treatment, there must also be a degree of overlap: the point of intellectual debate added to the counterpoint of historical exposition.

1. Superior figures throughout refer to Bibliographical references, pp. 115-28.

I

THE RISE OF THE PRINCES

Our starting point is with the figure of the secular ruler as he began to dominate European politics in the second half of the fifteenth century. The prince was of course far from being a newcomer to the scene, having long divided the western world with the papacy and upheld the noble ideal of Christendom. But, as the power of that great unifying concept diminished, he took on a new lease of life and, at the expense of alternative political forms, imposed his own authority. Late fifteenth — and early sixteenth — century Europe was not entirely the domain of princes: there was a republic still in Venice, though after her neighbour, Florence, had become the prince's greatest trophy there could be no doubting the truth of Burckhardt's lament that the republics' star was in decline.[1] The bright light of the High Renaissance reveals the political face of Europe caught in a gallery of princely portraits. Everywhere his public appearances acquired a theatrical character, as increasingly the prince acted out his role in a carefully contrived spotlight against sumptuous backcloths and with a cast of supporting players, so that his easy and natural domination of the stage was immediately apparent to the audience. He succeeded spectacularly and almost universally in searing his subjects' minds with a deferential mark which would not be readily erased. And in relations between states the political life of Europe began to throb to the pulse of the royal courts.

Even on the distant margin of Europe the renaissance of

princely power was palely reflected in the court of the grand dukes of Muscovy. There the aspiring Ivan the Great, unabashed by the Turkish conquest of Constantinople in 1453, succeeded in marrying Sophia Palaeologue, niece of the last eastern emperor, who brought a dowry of Byzantine ritual and ceremonial upon which Ivan was not slow to capitalise. In the words of the first great Russian historian, Karamzin, he sought 'to bring Greece back to life in Russia by observing all her ecclesiastical and courtly ceremonials. He surrounded himself with Roman eagles, and received foreign ambassadors in the *Golden Chamber* which recalled that of Justinian. . . . Ikon painters, engravers and goldsmiths grew rich in our capital city'.[2] To this hybrid court, without evident enthusiasm, came the Venetian ambassador, Contarini: 'On the 22nd September, 1476, it pleased God that we should enter Russia'.[3] The account of his subsequent reception indicates the relatively informal atmosphere which still prevailed in the Kremlin despite obvious efforts to make an impression. Contarini was invited to the palace to dine with the duke and before dining was received in audience. This private meeting lasted over an hour and, despite the ambassador's initial attempt to observe the etiquette which he felt the occasion demanded, the two men were soon conversing easily. Before the audience came to an end Ivan was showing off some of his most beautiful garments of cloth of gold, ermine-lined, to his duly gratified guest. They then repaired to the banquet chamber for the formal dinner with its profusion of dishes, held in the presence of many boyars. At its conclusion the grand duke took his official leave of the ambassador, speaking in a loud voice so that everybody could hear, and adding diplomatic expressions of goodwill towards the Venetian Republic. The proceedings ended with the presentation to Contarini of a large silver goblet filled with mead and the invitation to drink the contents and keep the cup. No doubt to his chagrin, for the gesture was a mark of very great honour, Contarini found himself unable to drink more than a quarter. However, observing his predicament, Ivan gallantly ordered the cup to be emptied and restored to the abstemious envoy.[4]

By the following reign, of Vasili III, a more elaborate, formal and stage-managed procedure had evolved to which the ambassador of the Holy Roman Emperor was subjected in 1526:

We entered the apartments in the company of those who had joined us last. In the first of them people were dressed in velvet or silk ornamented with gold; from these come the men chosen at any moment for important posts. We went into a second room, coming after this into the presence-chamber. . . . The presence of so many people on such a day, summoned to the castle and herded into it, arises from two causes: so that foreigners may note the size of the crowd and the mightiness of its lord and also so that vassals may note the respect in which their master is held, being visited by such great potentates in the persons of their respected ambassadors. . . . The Grand-duke's throne is higher by a hand's length than the tabouret. . . . In front of him was a very low bench, covered with a carpet, upon which the envoys sat.[5]

Finally, at the court of Ivan the Terrible, grandson of Ivan the Great and first tsar of Muscovy, all the grandiose allusions of the western princes were matched and, if we are to believe Richard Chancellor's account, in some respects exceeded. Chancellor's arrival in Moscow following his shipwreck *en route* to China was the occasion of a royal reception and banquet. In view of the subsequent trading arrangements between Muscovy and England arising out of this visit, we may assume that the opportunity was taken to impress the Englishman. Clearly he was dazzled by the extravagance of the gold and silver plate and by the richness of the apparel, the tsar himself wearing three different crowns during the course of the proceedings. However, there was also a routine ceremonial element which clearly demonstrated the effectiveness of the royal cult of personality. First of all, at his reception, Chancellor noted how

the interpretour came for me into the utter [*sic*] chamber, where sate one hundred or more gentlemen, all in cloth of golde very sumptuous, and from thence I came into the Counsaile chamber, where sate the Duke himselfe with his nobles, which were a faire company: they sate round about the chamber on high, yet so that he himselfe sate much higher than any of his nobles in a chaire gilt, and in a long garment of beaten golde, with an emperial crowne upon his head, and a staffe of Cristall and golde in his right hand. . . .[6]

Even more significant was the procedure adopted throughout the banquet, whereby from his position of solitary splendour:

The Duke sent to every man a great shiver [*sic*] of bread, and the bearer called
the party so sent to by his name aloude, and sayd, Ivan Vasilevich Emperour
of Russia and great Duke of Moscovia doth reward thee with bread: then must
all men stand up, and doe at all times when those words are spoken.[7]

During his stay Chancellor also had the opportunity to observe
the tsar as a warlord, 'richly attired above all measure; his pavilion
is covered either with cloth of gold or silver, and so set with
stones that it is wonderfull to see it. I have seene the Kings
Majesties of England and the French Kings pavilions, which are
fayre, yet not like unto his.'[8] From one who was old enough to
recall the Field of the Cloth of Gold, this was a compliment
indeed.

Western princes were no less anxious than their Russian
counterparts to amaze the world with their might, but the
character of their regimes was different: for the opulence of the
house of Rurik was still redolent of the unbridled barbarism of
Genghis Khan, while that of the western dynasties was woven
into sophisticated ideals of chivalrous and courtly behaviour
which were most elaborately and impressively demonstrated at
the court of the dukes of Burgundy. There the atmosphere was
as regal as in Moscow. The duke held a public audience on
Mondays and Fridays with a great display of pageantry, surrounded by princes of the blood, knights and ambassadors and by
his own liveried attendants who conducted each performance
through its well-rehearsed routine. Prominent on this, as on all
other public occasions, were the knights of the Golden Fleece
whose order, founded in 1430 by Duke Philip the Good, represented all that was considered virtuous and seemly at that brilliant
court. Indeed, classical heroes like Jason and Ulysses were much
admired and the cult of Hercules in particular became a dominant
motif.[9]

Burgundian court life offered a rich, dramatic spectacle with
moments of intoxicating splendour like the wedding of Charles
the Bold, the last native duke, to Margaret of York in 1468. On
that occasion the festivities lasted for ten days during which time

sumptuous banquets were interspersed with moralising tableaux representing the twelve labours of Hercules, each extolling some aspect of the Burgundian code:

To his great credit Hercules succeeded in slaying the fierce monster which sought as its prey Hesion, the beautiful daughter of the great king of Troy; and in giving peace, tranquillity and joy to the people. O valiant knights and noblemen, learn from this example: Hercules urges you to do so. Show great boldness in protecting virtuous ladies. Wield your arms with becoming valour. Defend their honour which is their most priceless possession. Any who act otherwise offend against nobility.[10]

But the centre-piece of the celebrations was a protracted tournament held before the ducal pair and their wedding guests. Knights from England, France and Germany, Italy and Burgundy entered the lists: the son of the prince of Orange, the brother of the constable of France, two brothers of the English queen and a host of other combatants vied with each other in the ornateness of their horses' trappings, the prodigality of their pages' apparel and the number and quality of their attendants. Day after day they proudly paraded themselves in the dangerous mock-heroic ritual of the joust, and the broken lances littering the floor of the great market-place in Bruges testified to the fierceness of their endeavours. This was the court from which other European rulers would draw their inspiration and at which the future Emperor Charles V, great grandson of the newly-married couple of 1468, would pass the days of his youth.

By that time, in the first decades of the sixteenth century, the influence of Italian humanism was being felt in northern Europe, adding another dimension to the character of the prince. To the courtly image was added that of the connoisseur of letters, the cultivated patron of the arts: princes were admonished to pay at least as much regard to the letters of Homer as to the arms of Achilles.[11] From this marriage of Italy and Burgundy sprang a breed of super-princes whose prestige and authority, reflected in the physical, moral and intellectual attributes of their own persons, made them appear as demi-gods. Before ascending the French throne the future Francis I requested the Italian diplomat, Baldassare Castiglione, to compose a treatise, which though primarily intended for the guidance of courtiers, was effectively dominated by the awe-inspiring personality of the prince. That remains so even after account has been taken of Castiglione's natural inclination to favour his patron, of whom he writes in glowing terms:

> For it is not long sins I was in France, and saw this Prince in the Court there, who seemed unto mee beside the handsomnesse of person and bewtie of visage, to have in his countenance so great a majestie, accompanied neverthelesse with a certaine lovely courtesie, that the realme of Fraunce shoulde ever seeme unto him a small matter. I understood afterwarde by many gentlemen both French and Italian, verie much of the most noble conditions, of the greatnesse of courage, prowesse and liberalitie that was in him: and among other things, it was tolde me, that hee highly loved and esteemed letters, and had in very great reputation all learned men. . . .[11]

But he was no less impressed by the other two members of the great triumvirate, the future Charles V, who 'will darken the name of many Emperors of olde time, and in renowne be compared to the most famous that ever were in the world', and the future Henry VIII, 'the Lorde Henry prince of Wales, who presently groweth under his most noble father, in all kind of vertue, like a tender Impe under the shadow of an excellent tree . . . nature was willing in this prince to shew her cunning, in one bodie alone so many excellent vertues, as were sufficient to decke out infinit.'[13] Nor did he forget the princes of his native Italy or the late Queen Isabella of Castile.

Not even the dispassionate legal eye of the French humanist-lawyer Guillaume Budé could detect a different image, and that he should deny any trace of adulation or ostentation in his portrait of Francis I suggests that his mind was sharply focused upon his subject. He listed the qualities of mind and body with which he believed the king was endowed: a good memory and understanding, discreet judgment, a lively imagination, innate courtesy, good health, a sturdy frame and an imposing, even a truly heroic, stature, remarkable agility and dexterity, a comely demeanour, an air of elegance and majesty, a natural fluency in conversation. In a more succinct comment on the king's virtues Budé underlined the Burgundian influence, 'Et serez au temps avenir le roy surnommé "Musegètes" qui était au temps passé le surnom de Phebus ou Hercules. . . '.[14] Indeed the cult of Hercules prospered in royal propaganda as in French literature, and the intermingling of Burgundian and Italian ideas may be observed in the tableau forming part of the ceremonial entry of Francis's queen, Eleanor, into Rouen in 1532, in which the king was referred to as 'nouvel Hercules lequel a fait fleurir en ce Royaume les langues hebraïque, grecque, latine, italienne, espagnole et germaine, mêmement la française qui par avant était assez champêtre.'[15]

Some six years before this paragon ascended the French throne in 1515, the 'tender Impe' across the channel succeeded his father as Henry VIII, and in every way the new king of England compared favourably with his future French rival. Henry VII was less flamboyant than his son, but he had chosen, nevertheless, to act out his public role in a richly decorative court, and this court now blossomed even more spectacularly under the touch of the second Tudor. In many ways it was reminiscent of Burgundy. As a young prince, Henry became a devotee of the tournament and remained so throughout his active life. Always avid for the joust he was *Cœur Loyal* who would take on all comers and usually prevail, a dashing, impressive figure of a man, strong as an ox and superbly athletic: as worthy as Sir Lancelot to be called 'the courteoust knight that ever bare shield'.[16]

There was another side, of course, to Henry: the polymath prince, who knew Latin, Greek, French and Italian, was an apt student of mathematics and a considerable musician. For the arch-humanist Erasmus, therefore, the English court was 'a temple of the Muses':

the seat and citadel of the best studies . . . where under princely favour Good Letters are dominant, the love of Honour is strong, and a sentence of banishment has been passed against that futile and tasteless learning with its masked affectation of holiness, which used to be in fashion with uneducated men of education.[17]

By this combination of chivalrous and cerebral virtues Henry established an awesome hold over his subjects' imagination.

Drawing upon his own experience of royal service Sir Thomas Smith declared in 1565 that:

> the prince is the life, the head and the authoritie of all thinges that be doone in the realme of England. And to no prince is doone more honor and reverence than to the King and Queene of Englande, no man speaketh to the prince nor serveth at the table but in adoration and kneeling, all persons of the realme be bareheaded before him: insomuch that in the chamber of presence where the cloath of estate is set, no man dare walke, yea though the prince be not there, no man dare tarrie there but bareheaded.[18]

On a smaller scale Italy itself, with its mosaic of princely courts, offered a similar picture, reflecting both the humanistic ideals of kingship which had spread to northern Europe and the aura of Burgundian bravura which was having its effect in the south as well. Between 1470 and 1475 firm political links were established between Italy and Burgundy when first the Venetians and then the king of Naples and the duke of Milan sent resident envoys to Charles the Bold, while long-established commercial links were maintained by men like Portinari, who represented the Florentine Medici bank in Bruges.[19] The chivalrous and courtly ideal was implanted in the peninsula at courts like that of the Gonzaga of Mantua, the Este family of Ferrara with their Order of the Golden Spur, at Urbino, later the setting for Castiglione's *Courtier,* whose duke, together with the king of Naples and the duke of Ferrara, were honoured by the English court as knights of the Garter, and at the Sforza court of Milan, the latter claimed by Burckhardt to be, under Ludovico the Moor, the most brilliant since the heyday of the Burgundian court itself.[20] Like their more powerful northern counterparts, each of them strove to be 'an accomplished ruler, captain and gentleman', and though they were large fish operating in a small pond some of them nevertheless achieved a kind of immortality by association: one recalls Lorenzo the Magnificent's patronage of the young Michelangelo and Leonardo's lengthy stay at the court of Ludovico Sforza.[21]

The same pattern may be picked out in other parts of Europe too. In Heidelberg, at the court of successive rulers of the Palatinate, the knightly reputation of Frederick the Victorious

(1449–76), acclaimed in the Burgundian manner by specially commissioned court historians, gave way to the gentler humanistic arts of Philip the Upright (1476–1508) who attracted into his orbit such famous writers and teachers as Agricola, Reuchlin and Wimpfeling, so that it is possible to assert that 'the mechanism of patronage and the lively personal involvement of princes were remarkably similar in Italy, southern Germany and Burgundy in the late fifteenth century'.[22] In Poland too, at the court of Sigismund I (1506–40) and his queen Bona Sforza, the warrior prince revealed himself, yet again in the Renaissance mould, as a patron of the arts and a student of classical antiquity, mathematics and music. Finally, in Hungary the Renaissance ruler was spectacularly portrayed in the person of Mátyás Corvinus (1458–90). He was a soldier of rare talent, a notable linguist and the owner of a library known to scholars all over Europe. Like Sigismund of Poland he too had marital links with the world of the Italian Renaissance through his second wife, Beatrix, a daughter of the king of Naples. Under his charismatic leadership Hungary was rescued from the triple threat of Turkish, Imperial and Czech domination and Buda became an artistic and intellectual centre to rival the capitals of Italy.[23]

All over Europe then, the prince was coming to dominate the scene and one may ask how such a virtuoso performance could be sustained. In the first place it was sustained by an appeal to the divine element in his office, for no ruler, however worldly the setting in which he chose to display himself, could contemplate challenging the ultimate spiritual values which overshadowed the exercise of his secular power. On the contrary, princes began to edge closer to the Divinity to add the necessary spiritual panache to their temporal glory. Francis I's reign began with a new arrangement between himself and the Pope — the Concordat of Bologna (1516) — which would involve the Crown even more intimately than before in the affairs of the French church and ended with a number of literary allusions to the divine apotheosis of departed monarchs.[24] There were further echoes of this princely preoccupation in two great European monuments, both under the patronage of Saint Laurence, the Escorial in Spain, a royal palace, monastery and tomb, and the Medici chapel in the church of San Lorenzo in Florence, Michelangelo's memorial to that city's ruling house. In Muscovy, the native prince and the Greek patriarch had parted company, leaving the Grand Duke with the awesome responsibility of preserving intact that rare brand of Orthodox Christianity which was evolving in Moscow, the third Rome. Herberstein observed that, for his audience with Vasili III in 1526, the Grand Duke had at his left hand 'a bowl with two small jugs and towel on top of them. He is said to maintain that when he offers his hand to one of the Roman faith it is defiled; thus as soon as the envoy has moved away he washes his hands and cleanses them'.[25] 'God knows and the Grand Duke' was how the pious Muscovite acknowledged this special relationship.[26]

It was not, however, simply a matter of the eccentricity of individual rulers: all of them were aware of the solemn responsibilities which went with such proximity to the Almighty, and if they momentarily forgot there was usually somebody close at hand to remind them. Philippe de Commynes, an old servant of Louis XI of France, put the matter in these apocalyptic terms:

... who will inform against the mighty and bring their evidence before a judge and who will be the judge to punish the evildoers? I reply that the evidence will be the lamentation and the clamour of the people whom they grind down and oppress in so many ways without compassion or pity; the grievous wailing of widows and orphans whose husbands and fathers they have caused to die and who are left to mourn; in general, all those suffering persecution in body or through their possessions. That will be the evidence and their loud cries for justice and pitiable tears will bring them to the attention of Our Lord, the proper judge of such matters. . . .[27]

No French king would have been surprised at such strictures since *le roi très chrétien* had long felt himself obliged to govern in accordance with God's commandments, to preside over a regime which would reflect divine justice, to represent the Almighty on French soil. Was he not consecrated with holy oils at his coronation and did he not claim miraculous powers of healing as a concomitant of his quasi-spiritual role? Consequently he was expected, in the words of Claude de Seyssel, another servant of the French royal house writing in 1515, to make it known by example and by visible and outward signs that he was a zealot, an observer of the Faith and of the Christian religion, and that he was resolved to use his power to sustain and strengthen it.[28] Such obligations might limit the king's freedom of action but they also added considerable weight to his authority and lustre to his reputation.

But the cosmopolitan Erasmus was admonishing all European rulers when he wrote,

If you are a Prince . . . consider that this is the right of it: Christ Jesus is the one Lord of all. You should emulate as best you can Him whom you naturally serve as a deputy. No-one should observe His teachings more scrupulously than you, from whom He will exact a more stringent accounting than from others.[29]

The same theme was echoed by another much-travelled figure, Castiglione. 'It is God, therefore, that hath appointed the people under the custody of princes, which ought to have a diligent care over them, that they may make him account of it, as good stewardes doe their Lorde . . .'.[30] Erasmus also addressed himself on the subject specifically to Henry VIII, reminding him of his exceptional position as an image of the Deity, an image sedulously fostered by Henry who, resenting the honorific titles of his rivals, the Most Christian King of France and His Catholic Majesty of Spain, worked hard to extract from the pope his own style of 'Defender of the Faith'.[31]

In the Russian world, 'the much sinning and poor slave of God',[32] Ivan the Great, began to consolidate the alliance of church and state out of which grew the influential idea that, following the failure of Rome and Constantinople to preserve inviolate the Christian religion, that task had fallen to Moscow alone and to the grand duke in particular. The extent to which the secular ruler subsequently identified himself with the religious life of his country and became in fact a spiritual personage, is strikingly illustrated by the correspondence of Ivan the Terrible with his erstwhile *boyar* friend, Michael Kurbsky. His role, maintained Ivan, was to 'endeavour with zeal to guide people to the truth

and to the light in order that they may know the one true God . . .
and the sovereign given to them by God; and in order that they
may cease from internecine strife and a froward life, which things
cause kingdoms to crumble'.[33] His sense of personal responsibility
for the moral welfare of his subjects went deeper than with any
of his western counterparts: 'I therefore believe that I as a servant
shall receive judgment for all my sins . . . and not only for my own
sins but for those of my subjects shall I answer, should any sin be
committed because of my remissness'.[34]

One effect of this commitment to a politico-religious ideal saw
that wars in which Muscovy was involved were represented as
Holy Wars waged on behalf of Russian Orthodoxy. 'The
German towns wait not for the clash of arms but bow down their
heads at the appearance of the life-giving cross', claimed Ivan the
Terrible, and again, 'the advancing banner inscribed with the
Cross had no need of any military cunning, as not only Russia,
but also the Germans and Lithuania and the Tatars and many
peoples know; . . . they were not my victories but God's'.[35] In
this however he was not first in the field, his wily grandfather
having previously taken the same line against Lithuania.[36] In the
west too, there were those who believed that war could only be
justified as a crusade against the infidel. Thus Erasmus, who
thought it 'so brutish, as that it becomes beasts rather than men;
. . . so licentious, that it stops the course of all justice and honesty
. . . and so unchristian, that it is contrary to the express commands
of the gospel', nevertheless praised Sigismund of Poland for his
campaigns against the Turk and Budé made an exception to his
general prohibition in favour of Christian princes who made war
'contre les infidèles pour augmenter la foy catholicque et
orthodoxe . . .'.[37] And at precisely the moment that Ivan III was
pursuing his crusade against Lithuania in the east, in the west a
Spanish chronicler was recording the triumphant conclusion of
another Holy War with the fall of the Moorish city of Granada
and the last dramatic act of the whole *reconquista,* when Spanish
knights entered the Alhambra and:

displayed on the highest tower, first the standard of Jesus Christ, which was
the Holy Cross that the king carried always with him in this holy undertaking;

and he and the queen and the prince and all the host bent low before the Holy Cross and gave great thanks and praise to Our Lord; and the archbishops and clergy said the Te Deum Laudamus. . . .[38]

The prince also sought to justify his role by emphasising that his credentials were based on a tradition of authority which he would continue to respect and support. Machiavelli was dogmatic in his assertion that hereditary rulers, even those of only average capacity, were unlikely to experience much difficulty in maintaining their position provided that they did not transgress their predecessors' customs and were not peculiarly endowed with vices.[39] For that same reason Emperor Charles V was untroubled at the prospect of handing over the Spanish crown to his son Philip, who, in inheriting the kingdom, would join a line of succession at once fixed, secure and ancient.[40] Machiavelli was of course too much of a realist to ignore the fact that, especially in Italy, rulers possessing this hereditary qualification were not thick on the ground; nevertheless he insisted that to be successful new men had not only to combine the qualities of the lion and the fox, like the Roman Emperor Severus, but more specifically should retain the laws and ancient customs under which their subjects were accustomed to live, or at least the semblance of the old forms, for 'the great majority of mankind are satisfied with appearances, as though they were realities'.[41]

In fact, power could not be bought simply through the condottiere's professional skill; the prince had to acquire his own aura of legitimacy if his guarantees were to be effective. For some, such an aura was not easily captured, though all of them worked hard at the task. The Bentivoglio in Bologna, the Malatesta in Rimini, the Petrucci in Sienna, the Visconti in Milan and, most strikingly of all, the Medici in Florence continued to govern through inherited constitutional machinery, while Ludovico Sforza, whose family succeeded the last of the Visconti, professed his intention of respecting the liberties of his great vassals, at the same time requiring them to defer to the rights of others.[42] In Italy, where Venice continued to represent the old civic virtues and Florentine republicans fought a series of battles with their Medici overlords, there was a special premium on legitimacy. The new princes employed artists and architects to provide the splendour necessary to off-set the deficiencies of their ancestry. How significant such patronage may have been in promoting the Italian artistic renaissance is happily a question outside the bounds of the present discussion, though it is a fact that artists did become prominent figures in these courts and they did fulfil a political as well as an aesthetic function.[43]

Likewise the brilliance of other European courts reflected their princes' concern to demonstrate the legitimacy of their rule or to blot out the memory of a recent murky past. The early Tudors fostered the legend of King Arthur. Court poets like Bernadus Andreas and Giovanni de' Giglis embodied the myth in occasional verses, and court revels were shot through with Arthurian symbolism, so that by association the new dynasty might acquire a spurious antiquity with which to obscure the true meaning of Bosworth.[44] An even more bizarre genealogy was devised for the grand dukes of Muscovy by the author of the 'History of the Princes of Vladimir', writing in the first quarter of the sixteenth century, who claimed that they were descended from Prus, a mythical brother of Caesar Augustus, while an apologist of the Hungarian king, Mátyás Corvinos, did not shrink from linking his hero with the immortals by postulating his descent from Zeus.[47]

Such outlandish quests for political respectability draw attention in fact to that element of *force majeure,* of power politics, which princes sought to conceal but which perceptive contemporaries observed to be growing at the beginning of the early modern period in long-established, as in short-lived principalities. However, the significance of such a development cannot be accurately gauged without first attempting to discover what role these princes were expected to play in the states over which they ruled and what concept they had of the state itself.

2

THE LIMITS AND IMPLICATIONS OF
PRINCELY AUTHORITY

In seeking answers to the questions raised at the end of the last chapter one can do no better than begin by consulting Machiavelli, the most profound contemporary analyst of princely politics. When he wrote about the state he used the expression to denote a variety of ideas: the power of the ruler and the machinery for its enforcement; the complex of rights and obligations to which he laid claim; and the geographical extent of his lands.[1] It is most important to note, however, that all these ideas had something in common: the assumption that the existence of the state depended on the prior existence of the prince, a patrimonial, dynastic outlook which was as fundamental to the sixteenth century as it was irrelevant to the nineteenth. According to this view the ruler inherited the state as a landowner inheriting his father's property, save that his possessory authority lay in the power to act rather than in ownership of the land itself (except for those domains within the state which belonged personally to him). Thus the Venetian Contarini could observe in a matter-of-fact way that Moscow belonged to Duke Ivan III, the sovereign of Great White Russia, and Ivan himself in his last testament ordered the inheritance of his lordship of Muscovy as though it were a piece of real estate. 'I bless my oldest son, Vasiliy, with my patrimony, the grand principalities, with which my father blessed me and which God gave me.'[2] Similar sentiments echoed across Europe. In France Budé elaborated the metaphor of the king-paterfamilias acting under divine orders:

> . . . nothing is to be more esteemed or marvelled at than the knowledge whereby an individual can duly and honourably govern himself and his family, a knowledge even more necessary for those with a larger family, a family too numerous to be counted, such as princes and kings possess; for their family covers the whole extent of their *seigneurie* and they are responsible not only for their own family, their servants and officers, but also for all those under their jurisdiction for whom they must answer to God who has committed them to their charge. . . .[3]

In Italy Don Scipio di Castro pursued the image of the prince as father and pastor, and at the moment of abdicating the Spanish crown the Emperor Charles V reminded his son of the need to act with paternal bounty, as shepherd to his flock.[4] Some little time later, that most articulate of monarchs, James I, reiterated the now familiar statement of patrimonial kingship which allocated to the prince the role of 'careful watchman' of his patrimony and 'naturall father and kindly master' of his people.[5] And because state-concepts did not develop simultaneously all over Europe, this traditional interpretation of the state as a royal patrimony still lingered on in the German Empire at the close of the seventeenth century. The Elector Frederick William I of Brandenburg-Prussia was so under its sway that he sought in his last will to divide the state between his six sons. Without a doubt the prince's chief objective and interest, like that of any careful husband-man, was to preserve his state's integrity, extending its boundaries if possible, but ensuring at least that he bequeathed his patrimony undiminished.

The chief domestic preoccupation of princes was, in James I's words, that of 'maintaining and putting to execution the olde lowable lawes of the countrey, and . . . establishing of new (as necessitie and evil maners will require)'. This judicial role, though concerned with the provision of security and political stability, was essentially passive. It consisted primarily in holding the ring, in recognising and maintaining the pattern of customary rights and privileges belonging to their subjects into which their own authority was inextricably woven. That is why James I talked of the need 'to maintaine the whole countrey, and every state therein, in all their ancient Priviledges and Liberties',[6] and such sentiments had been commonplace for more than a hundred years. Seyssel recognised the preservation of justice as the prince's proper function but he pointed out too that he should not trespass on the rights and prerogatives of his subjects without good cause and lengthy deliberation, a prohibition also applied to the ministers of the Spanish king by Charles V.[7] For Guicciardini, 'The fruit of liberties and the end for which they were instituted is not government by everyone — for only the able and deserving should govern — but the observance of just laws and order'.[8] Thomas More believed that kings should hesitate to enforce any law fallen into desuetude particularly when no adverse effect could be discerned upon the subjects, and Machiavelli too concentrated on the passive aspect of princely justice: 'It makes him [the prince] hated above all things as I have said, to be rapacious, and to be a violator of the property and women of his subjects, from both of which he must abstain. And when neither their property nor honour is touched, the majority of men live content'.[9] He referred on a number of occasions, with obvious approval, to the example of France where the king 'has bound himself by a number of laws that provide for the security of all his people'.[10]

There were also other elements which contributed to the overall concept of the ruler's judicial role as it was understood during the sixteenth century. He should not act without taking counsel from the wisest heads in his kingdom, men with an obligation to speak honestly and without flattery, but he should remain the final arbiter and should seek to outgrow his counsellors in wisdom. He was also the fount of distributive justice, bestowing honours and profits upon those subjects whose services rendered them worthy and who were thus bound more firmly in loyalty to their prince, as were all subjects, like those of the Catholic kings, who witnessed that rewards were granted proportionately to the merits and not the birth of the recipients.[11] There was another element too which embraced both distributive justice and the necessity to take advice. This was the need to govern by the light of reason, an aspect of the prince's role that requires further explanation.

This idea was bound up with the ruler's need to study and learn from experience so that, in a Platonic sense, he might glimpse that essential justice which would govern his actions. 'Law', observed Erasmus, 'is a reflection of the absolute idea of Right',[12] and it was incumbent upon the prince to acquire sufficient wisdom to perceive the idea. To achieve that objective, disinterested advisors and sound counsel, though important, were not sufficient; the ruler was expected to make his own contribution as well. He should become an historian, learning how some monarchies had fallen, how others had maintained their power and prosperity for so long. He should follow the advice of Philip of Macedon to his son Alexander and study the works of Aristotle, for political science was another important guide along the road to sagacity. He should also learn the lessons of his own experience and see to it that he chose, as ministers and advisors, men who likewise fashioned their conduct according to such precepts.[13] In a word the prince should 'apply all his studie and diligence to get knowledge, afterwarde to fashion within himselfe and observe unchangeably in every thing the law of reason . . . that it may be to him alwaies not only familiar, but inwarde, and live with him as a parcell of him'. However, Castiglione also asserted in the same breath that 'It is God therefore that hath appointed the people under the custody of princes',[14] a reminder that the quest for perfect justice was not only borrowed from the authors of classical antiquity, whose works were enjoying such a potent revival in western Europe. It was also Christian in inspiration, a search for the shadow of divine justice on earth. No sooner had Budé cited Plato's famous remark that happiness in this world depended on wise men becoming kings or kings wise men, than he invoked the Almighty as the only source of such a felicitous conjunction.[15]

Yet there was in this doctrine of political reason something that did not derive from either the classical or the Christian tradition but was nevertheless to assume crucial significance in the course of time: this was the idea, still inchoate at the beginning of the sixteenth century, that wisdom and justice were not absolute virtues but had to be related to the political needs of the moment. When that happened, what was formerly considered virtue might assume an odd appearance and what was vice, a new disguise. Although Budé wrote of both 'Justice' and 'Wisdom' his favourite word was 'Discretion'.[16] The Italian Scipio di Castro, in cataloguing the virtues which would be revealed to the prince by the light of reason included the following: an understanding of his subjects' nature, the wisdom to make laws, the ability to assess men's services, art in making war, industry in preserving peace, judgment in weighing up the posture of other states, skill in temporising with inconveniences, maturity in deliberation, swiftness in execution, constancy in resolution, valour in misadventure, moderation in triumph, so assured a knowledge in matters of divinity that neither superstition would make him timorous nor presumption adventurous.[17] Here reason and religion still go together and solid Christian virtues still outweigh any other implicit attributes of kingship. Perhaps such attributes were hinted at in Machiavelli's observation that 'men in their conduct, and especially in their most prominent actions, should well consider and conform to the times in which they live' and in Charles V's remark that those who govern states must adapt themselves to opportunities and circumstances.[18]

So far we have considered the ruler–subject relationship entirely from the prince's point of view; it remains to discover what part, if any, the subject was expected to play in the business of government and to what extent his interests were likely to shape government policy. The short answer is that his voice was of little relevance in such matters, for his role—reflecting that of the prince in domestic affairs—was essentially passive. He was part of a judicial organisation which provided him with an assured place and reduced the likelihood of civil disturbance, and he was protected from external aggression by the ruler's armed forces. He was thus free to pursue his own legitimate interests—which included everything not inimical to the established order —in the relative security of an established polity. Any idea that he should play an active part in the maintenance of such a polity was unthought of by princes and unthinkable to impartial and articulate observers. To Seyssel the people were turbulent and dangerous, to Erasmus they were 'the unbridled masses, the tumultuous dregs of the state', and to Guicciardini, 'To speak of the people is to speak of a madman, a monster full of confusion and errors, whose vain opinions are as far from the truth as Spain, according to Ptolemy, is from India'.[19] Yet, for all that, they did exercise a considerable indirect influence upon the ruler both in moral terms, for the holder of a patrimony bore a kind of paternal responsibility for those under his authority, and in another respect too: if he failed to govern justly, the prince could not depend on his subjects' loyalty and then he could also easily become a prey to hostile neighbours. Machiavelli repeatedly stressed the importance, for the ruler, of not sacrificing the people's good-will. He dismissed the proverb that 'He who builds on the people builds on the mud', alleging on the contrary that 'the best possible fortress is—not to be hated by the people, because, although you may hold the fortresses, yet they will not save you if the people hate you, for there will never be wanting foreigners to assist a people who have taken arms against you'. Once more Charles V echoed the Italian's sentiments, advising his son that without the application of royal justice to safeguard the subjects' honour, life and property, all the arms and fortresses in the world could not maintain the state in peace and harmony.[20] Justice, as we have seen, was pre-eminently concerned with respecting the rights and privileges of the various groups and estates of the realm or principality. Within that definition there was one sphere in which it behoved princes to act with particular circumspection—that of finance. It was not considered just for them to raise taxes outside their family domains unless the circumstances were extraordinary—and that invariably meant in times of war—and unless their subjects were agreeable. Even if it was impossible to consult the people formally some token arrangement should be made and the reason for the extra taxation should be made clear.

Philippe de Commynes, who had observed the problem from close at hand, wrote in his *Mémoires*:

Therefore, to continue my discourse, is there any king or *seigneur* on earth who has the power, outside his own domain, to levy a single farthing from his subjects without the agreement and consent of those who have to pay, except by resorting to tyranny and violence? One might argue that there are times when it is not necessary to await an assembly, that it would take too long to arrange such a gathering when a war had to be fought. . . . Yet there can be no occasion, whatever the urgency, when it is not possible to call together some important people and say to them: 'This measure is not being taken without due cause', thereby eliminating fabrication and the strategem of embarking on a capricious and purposeless campaign in order to justify the levying of money.[21]

Similarly the prince should always distinguish carefully between public funds and his own resources, unlike Lorenzo the Magnificent in Florence, whose bad financial management forced him to dip into public money and even into the private fortunes of individual citizens, with a consequent adverse effect upon his reputation.[22]

For the rest, princes were expected to be sensitive to their subjects' interests, not imposing high tariffs on staple exports for example, like grain from Sicily or wine and silk from Naples, nor on vital imports either; on the contrary, by encouraging trade they could help to enrich their subjects and thereby make more money available to the royal exchequer in critical times. By the same token, heavy taxes on luxury goods were considered equitable since they did not affect the mass of the people. Wise rulers would follow the advice of Isabella d'Este who believed in their responsibility to provide grain for the needy in times of dearth. At the very least such a gesture, recalled to mind at a moment of financial exigency for the ruler, might provide the basis for a *quid pro quo*.[23] The prince should do everything in his power to nurse his subjects towards prosperity by providing the conditions of peace and stability in which they could pursue their enterprises. But he was not expected to take over his subjects' role except in so far as he required additional revenue to guarantee his state's security. Indeed, to do so would constitute 'crimen lese populi', the offence of which the Duke of Ferrara was allegedly guilty when he indulged in commerce, monopolies, 'and other vulgar things that ought to be done by private citizens'.[24]

The picture, so far delineated, of the princely state around the beginning of the sixteenth century is deficient in several important particulars: like the photograph of an athlete frozen in mid-stride it fails to take account of the tensions, the inner driving force, the essential movement denied in such a static representation. The missing elements are those of force and guile, dynamic factors which were quickly discerned by shrewd observers of the political scene, and were destined to transform the formal edifice which these same men had described. Nor need we be surprised at the importance of such elements since the prince's chief preoccupation turned out to be that of securing and maintaining his state against external aggression, an objective which suggests in itself that Renaissance Man had still some way to go before accepting to be governed by Attic ideals of perfect justice or simple Christian charity. In fact, international relations proved to be the chief catalyst for change in post-Renaissance Europe. This was so because the rise of the princes was constituted of a series of self-conscious proclamations of one dynasty's authority against another's.

Nowhere was this more evident than in Italy where the rivalry was intense and the room for manœuvre slight. One by one the weaker Italian states had succumbed to the great predators of the peninsula. Pisa fell to Florence, Cremona to Milan, and after 1425, when Venice committed herself to mainland affairs, so effectively did she adapt her republican constitution to the requirements of princely politics that, not only her neighbours in Ferrara, but also the most powerful men in Italy began to express alarm at her expansionist policies.[25] To achieve a kind of stability and order in this rapacious world, Italian rulers evolved the concept of a balance of power, a political equilibrium for which idea the Florentine historian, Guicciardini, gave most of the credit to his fellow countryman, Lorenzo de Medici: 'Knowing that it would be very dangerous to himself and to the Florentine Republic if any of the larger states increased their power, he diligently sought to maintain the affairs of Italy in such a balance that they might not favour one side more than another.'[26] An integral part of this new mechanistic approach to international affairs was the diplomat and it was the principality of Milan under Giangaleazzo Visconti which first revealed the capacity for sustained diplomatic activity as a means of achieving security, while Francesco Sforza's struggle for the Milanese succession in the mid-fifteenth century prompted the appearance of resident ambassadors throughout Italy.

Not surprisingly, therefore, Italian commentators had a good deal to say about the prince's need to secure his state against external aggression. 'The chief foundations of all states', claimed Machiavelli, ' . . . are good laws and good arms; and as there cannot be good laws where the state is not well armed, it follows that where they are well armed they have good laws.' He then capped this extremely dubious exercise in logic with one of those provocative and exaggerated pronouncements which, although subject to significant qualification when seen in the context of the whole work, nevertheless assured him of posthumous notoriety. He wanted to make the point abundantly clear that those rulers who neglected their frontiers, who in his own words thought more of ease than of arms, were courting political disaster: 'A prince ought to have no other aim or thought, nor select anything else for his study, than war and its rules and discipline.' He returned to the same subject in the *Discourses* and expressed much the same opinions.[27] His famous contemporary, Guicciardini, like Machiavelli an active politician as well as a distinguished observer, reflecting on these same *Discourses* and in particular upon the author's account of the rise of Rome, acknowledged that her lack of land and the fact that she was surrounded by powerful states left her no alternative but to advance her frontiers by whatever means were available, including force of arms. Regretfully he concluded that this was the pattern 'for those wishing to rule according to the common usage of the world, as they must; otherwise, being weak, they would be crushed and oppressed by their neighbours'.[28] Even Castiglione, that truly urbane figure who preached princely regard for the letters of Homer as well as for the arms of Achilles, did not doubt that the ruler should make his people warlike so that, he, and they, would have a sure defence against encroachment.[29] Meanwhile the pattern of Italian politics was being imitated in other parts of Europe as monarchs accepted the new diplomatic procedure as an additional means of guaranteeing the security of their realms. But the ambassadors, 'ces espions privilégiés entretenus mutuellement dans toutes les cours',[30] as Frederick II of Prussia was sneeringly, if accurately, to define them, still remained the personal agents of the prince, acting on his behalf in a sphere of fundamental importance to him, their loyalty immediate and personal. Thus when Ferdinand of Aragon chose not to answer his ambassador's despatches, they went unanswered, and that was an end to the matter, and when Henry VIII ascended the English throne he followed his father's example and chose Italian diplomats to act on his behalf.[31] Yet diplomacy did provide a safety valve as Europe contracted into a multitude of competing dynasties and the prince's prime obligation, to hand on his patrimony undiminished, became increasingly difficult to fulfil.

Sadly, however, the new diplomacy was much less potent than the forces which had called it into being, and, when Charles VIII led his troops into Lombardy in 1494, warfare was about to assume that leading role in European affairs which it has not relinquished since. Few then disputed the prince's need to fight, though some sought clarification of the just occasions of war. Claude de Seyssel, for example, who served Louis XII of France and lived long enough to pass on the fruits of his political experience to the youthful Francis I, counselled against wars waged to satisfy unworthy emotions, like the desire to dominate and the quest for glory. Yet on the other hand he supported those prosecuted by princes in defence of their own principalities or of allies, neighbours and friends under attack, and those undertaken to regain territory unjustly occupied by an enemy.[32] Francis's great rival, Charles V, had some reservations about the justice of war, though he was less explicit than Seyssel and the justification which he alleged, failure to obtain a solid and lasting peace by any other means, depended on a prior 'just cause' which he did not further define. In any case he clearly believed that war was inevitable, ineluctably bound up with the prince's obligation to conserve and if possible extend his realm. His son, Philip II, shared his father's determination to defend his God-given kingdoms though he was less convinced of the inevitability of conflict.[33] In England Sir Thomas Smith recognised the 'making of battell and peace, or truce with forraine nations' as one of the key functions of government, and so, unwillingly, did Richard Hooker towards the end of the sixteenth century. Later still, in his *Trew Law of Free Monarchies*, James I expressed his view of the twofold obligation of kingship, in which he coupled the maintenance of the law with the defence of the realm against foreign attack.[34]

There was more to all this, however, than the formal rituals of war and peace enacted between principalities: they merely disguised the element of force which some observers detected as crucial, not only in the sphere of international relations, but also in all political organisation. Machiavelli, whose name is indissolubly associated with these darker aspects of princely politics, understood the position better than most. He considered force to be at the very heart of the state, the ultimate guarantee of security in a dauntingly insecure situation. In the *Discourses* he periodically reminds his readers of that sense of inadequacy in man which begets recourse to violence: 'now, as people cannot make themselves secure except by being powerful . . .'; 'for fear to lose stirs the same passions in men as the desire to gain, as men do not believe themselves sure of what they already possess except by acquiring still more . . .'; 'for as some men desire to have more, whilst others fear to lose what they have, enmities and wars are the consequences'. In the *Prince* he acknowledges the inevitable consequence of this impulsion:

a prince, especially a new one, cannot observe all those things for which men are esteemed, being often forced, in order to maintain the state, to act contrary to fidelity, friendship, humanity and religion . . . let a prince have the credit of conquering and holding his state, the means will always be considered honest, and he will be praised by everybody.[35]

Machiavelli's uniqueness lay in the moral neutrality of his expression — what he perceived was shared by some of his contemporaries. 'Considering its origin carefully', concluded Guicciardini, 'all political power is rooted in violence.'[36] Erasmus chose to express a similar view in more emotional terms, referring in *In Praise of Folly* to those who 'found out the way how a man may draw his sword and sheathe it in his brother's bowels, and yet not offend against the duty of the second table, whereby we are obliged to love our neighbours as ourselves'. His friend Thomas More agreed that 'most kings are . . . more anxious, by hook or by crook, to acquire new kingdoms than to govern their existing ones properly', and the Frenchman, Seyssel, accustomed, like all these commentators, to observing the actions of princes at close hand, had also learnt to be cynical about human nature:

Since men are by nature corrupt and commonly so ambitious and anxious to achieve domination (even princes and others who govern great States) that one cannot simply take safety and security for granted, it is most necessary for all princes having the command and management of States at peace with their neighbours, to be always mindful of their needs and to maintain them at the ready.[37]

Sometimes direct force was replaced by guile. Seyssel, Guicciardini and Scipio di Castro all referred to the prince's exploitation of religion, the facility of appearing to have God on one's side, as 'a mask for the prince's own purposes'.[38] More wrote scathingly of the princes' lack of integrity and of the worthlessness of their most weighty undertakings:

. . . you can't rely on treaties at all. The more solemnly they're made, the sooner they're violated, by the simple process of discovering some loophole in the wording. . . . The implication seems to be that honesty is a low plebian virtue, far beneath the dignity of loyalty — or at least that there are two kinds of honesty. One is suitable for ordinary people, a plodding hack which is kept securely tethered, so that it can't go leaping any fences. The other, reserved for kings, is a far nobler animal which enjoys far greater freedom — for it's allowed to do exactly what it likes.[39]

Erasmus, who doubted whether the unvarnished truth was ever welcome to royal ears, criticised in particular that disguised force by which rulers exacted additional revenue from their subjects, invoking some title or other to give a pretence of justice to manifest extortion.[40]

Most revealing of all, however, is the testimony of Charles V, the last Holy Roman Emperor to maintain the Dantesque vision of an universal spiritual role, who abdicated his political authority to spend the concluding months of his life in preparation for eternity. One might have thought that he at least would tell a different story. Yet it was not so. In some respects he may have been an anachronism in the princes' world but he was of that world and he understood its ways well enough. In what was no doubt an old man's confession as well as a father's valediction to his son, Charles on the threshold of his abdication, wrote:

... the covetousness of men has carried them to such excesses and has so far exceeded the just limits within which they should contain themselves that the more possessions they have the more acquisitive they become. It is even looked upon as a mean act, a baseness of spirit, not only to give up what is superfluous but also not to employ every possible means to make new acquisitions daily.

In addition he considered war to be not only an inevitable part of human affairs but, from the prince's point of view, not altogether a bad thing. It kept soldiers occupied and prevented them from causing trouble at home; people paid their taxes more readily in wartime and formed the habit of paying, whereas in peacetime taxes had to be reduced and could only be reimposed with difficulty — war kept the state tuned up as exercise helps to keep the body fit.

As if in elaboration of these dubious principles Charles then outlined his proposals for dealing with threats from possible rivals, proposals that bore the clear imprint of opportunism. Against the French kingdom he favoured a head-on attack to prevent French intervention in Italy and he suggested to Philip that when hostilities had ended it should be possible to foment civil disorders within France from which the king of Spain could draw some profit. In the difficult matter of dealing with the papacy he proposed that if it was necessary to break with the pope Philip should broadcast the fact that he was not responsible and would much prefer to settle his differences through the intercession of mutual friends than by force of arms. As for the Venetians, Charles counselled tolerance in the expectation that they would ultimately fall victim to some bellicose prince who would subdue them without difficulty: 'Mais, si vous trouvez à propos de rompre avec eux, attaquez les brusquement. . . .'

Even in domestic matters his advice was sometimes couched in terms that later generations would call Machiavellian: the prince should hold long and frequent audiences, for people believe that they can lighten their burdens when they have the freedom to complain to their superiors; he should try to give some satisfaction if only kind words, to those who appeal to him; he must offer fine sounding reasons for demanding more money and then the people will willingly pay; it must appear that all favours emanate from the ruler, all unpopular policies from his ministers — a doctrine with a considerable future in Europe.[41]

How then may we reconcile these two coexisting aspects of princely government, the rule of the Christian prince soundly based upon universally accepted tenets of justice and law on the one hand, and the triumph of cut-throat opportunism, of *Realpolitik* on the other? The fact is, of course, that we have been studying a dynamic situation in which the very success of the prince was imperceptibly shaping and changing his role. This may best be seen in terms of his public and private capacities. It was still possible for Guicciardini, in discussing the Florentine rule of Lorenzo and Cosimo de Medici, to distinguish clearly between the public and private man: unlike Lorenzo, Cosimo always managed his business affairs so well that he had no need to borrow from public funds, his private fortune remaining greater than the income of the state. Yet the same author, writing later in his *Ricordi* on the subject of Ferdinand of Spain, acknowledges the advantages to be derived from confusing the two roles:

One of the greatest pieces of good fortune a man can have is the chance to make something he has done in his own interest appear to have been done for the common good. That was what made the enterprises of His Catholic Majesty so glorious. They were always undertaken for his own security or power, but often they would appear to be done either to strengthen the Christian faith or to defend the Church.

He then goes a stage further in claiming that princes, being ordained for the common good, had no right to hoard their revenues and profits, of which, properly speaking, they were only the administrators, but should employ them for the public good.[42] A similar ambiguity may be detected in the writings of Erasmus who in the *Enchiridion Militis Christiani* referred emphatically to the danger of the prince exploiting the public sector for private gain and turning freebooter, whilst reminding him in the same passage that 'You are a public figure and that you should not heed anything less than the public good'.[43] With the growth of the prince's public authority there was apparently little room left for his private role though it was not yet possible to dispense with it altogether; it remained as an undesirable alternative to his proper function. 'He that sits at the helm of government', wrote Erasmus, 'acts in a public capacity, and so must sacrifice all private interest to the attainment of the common good.'[44]

The most significant effect of this shift in the ruler's role was the new tendency, ill-defined but present nevertheless, to distinguish between public and private morality. While the prince as a private individual was held to be responsible to the Christian ethic, as a public personality, whose prime obligation lay in maintaining the security of his state, he might well have need of qualities which had nothing at all to do with Christianity. Thus the implications of force and guile in princely politics draw us into that same quickening current which we have already detected pulling at the foundations of the doctrine of political reason. To be sure, the current remained largely submerged: in the essential matter of whether the ruler was bound by the law, for example, there was no uniformity of opinion, though it is worth noting that Charles V evidently believed that he would only become subject to the law after his abdication.[45] There is one interesting piece of evidence however to be found in Seyssel's *La Monarchie de France*, in a section dealing with the prince's attitude in conquered countries where two factions exist. He takes the case in which one faction consistently opposes the conqueror and the other equally consistently takes his side. He concludes that in such a situation:

... in unimportant matters and in whatever is the concern of private suits they should be treated equally; but in matters of State and of great account and consideration preference must be given to those who take the Prince's side. For it is so much better to satisfy one group (that which favours lending its weight to the support and defence of the Prince) and to keep the other (which it is clear cannot be won over) so subdued that it cannot cause trouble, than to enfeeble and displease one's supporters and strengthen those whom one has no hope of gaining; so that with both sides disaffected they may easily join together against the Prince.

Seyssel undoubtedly found such counsel unpleasant to offer and in repeatedly stressing the importance of the prince's obligation to act according to precepts of justice, even when dealing with those individuals implacably opposed to him, he too was forced to take refuge in ambiguity. Proof of guilt must be clear, he insisted, if charges were to be proceeded with, and nobody should know that the prince had taken sides; nor ought he to do so if not — and here is the crucial phrase — 'pour autant qu'il est requis pour la sûreté de l'Etat'.[46]

Here it is important to bear in mind two significant points. First, that there was as yet no concept in Europe of the state as an entity distinct from both ruler and ruled — what we have observed is a tendency for the interests of the ruler and his state to become identical — and secondly, that this process worked from the top downwards and not vice-versa. Thomas More wryly remarked in *Utopia* that though people were always talking about the public interest they were really only concerned with private property, since they realised that if they did not protect their own interests they would starve to death, however prosperous the country in general might be.[47] Thus we should beware of misinterpreting aspects of the consolidation of princely authority in the late fifteenth and early sixteenth centuries as evidence of proto-national sentiment. Some historians have maintained that, in Spain, France and England in this period, signs of a community or proto-national spirit, fostered by an amalgam of religious, linguistic and geographical influences, can be detected. Yet in the context of the sixteenth century, when dynastic interests were so evidently to the fore, such an interpretation would seem to stand the facts on their head. While effective royal power continued to involve the maintenance of a variety of special rights and not a universal equality among subjects in relation to governmental authority, it can hardly be maintained that 'the modern democratic concept of the nation as a whole being "represented" began to take root'.[48] There was of course an element of community consciousness in Spain as elsewhere, 'founded on history, law and achievement, on the sharing of certain common experiences and certain common patterns of life and behaviour',[49] the product of centuries of political organisation, but the form of that organisation was sealed with a royal warrant. Thus Isabella, by her scrupulous adherence to judicial responsibilities and her zeal in taking fully into account her subjects' interests may have helped to focus their sense of identity, but such a policy was no more than their right and no less than her obligation. Neither in the relationship between them, nor in that between subject and ruler anywhere in Europe, was there the sign of a transformation.

The Spanish *reconquista* in particular has been interpreted in this light. Yet that crusade was surely a reflection of one of the deepest aspirations of Christendom, not a reflection of national sentiment. Successive Popes lent their support by levying a tax on the ecclesiastical establishments of Castile, Aragon and Sicily and thousands of volunteers from France, England, Germany, Switzerland, and even as far afield as Poland, joined the native Spaniards in the struggle for Granada, while Ferdinand's troops for the abortive attack on Tunis in 1511 contained a significant force of English archers.[50] The idea of the *respublica christiana* survived even the Reformation crisis; in 1565 English churchmen prayed for the Knights Hospitallers defending Malta and six years later Elizabeth I sent her congratulations to Philip II for the victory over the Turk at Lepanto, a victory that moved James VI of Scotland to poetry.[51] It was the ruler, not the ruled, who saw how this universal yearning might yield particular benefits to himself.

Again, the sixteenth century tendency to deprecate the employment of foreigners in a political and military capacity has been cited as further evidence of proto-nationalism. In her testament Isabella the Catholic of Spain called upon her successor to employ only Spaniards in government service, and as a result there was some reluctance to recognize Philip I as the new king until he had promised not to bring in foreign advisors. However, Isabella also incorporated into her will the reason for this prohibition: 'knowing that every kingdom has its laws and *fueros* and usages and customs and is governed better by its natives'.[52] In other words the paramount domestic obligation of government, to respect the multiplicity of the subjects' rights and privileges, was likely to be put at risk by officials who were not entirely familiar with the traditions of their adopted land. One of the stumbling blocks in Philip II's long battle against the Netherlands was his penchant for employing Spaniards in the Low Countries, men like Vargas, president of Alva's Council of Troubles, who made his scorn for local privileges abundantly clear.[53] James I, who ruled both Scotland and England, was keenly aware of the possibility of antagonising one country by setting over it, in the principal offices of state, natives of another who, from ignorance or malice, might fail to do it justice.[54] Civil government would not be possible, of course, without some mutual recognition of a common destiny and such recognition was basic to dynastic, princely rule for, as the guarantor of a variety of rights and liberties, the prince focused the aspirations of the community of his subjects.

A similar gloss is required to interpret opposition to mercenary troops as against a native force. Machiavelli in particular came back time and again to the argument in favour of the latter, citing his favourite example of the kingdom of France:

Charles VII . . . having by good fortune and valour liberated France from the English, recognised the necessity of being armed with forces of his own, and he established in his kingdom ordinances concerning men-at-arms and infantry. . . . The armies of the French have . . . become mixed, partly mercenary and partly national, both of which arms together are much better than mercenaries alone or auxiliaries alone, yet much inferior to one's own forces. And this example proves it, for the kingdom of France would be unconquerable if the ordinance of Charles had been enlarged or maintained.[55]

Machiavelli was expressing the basic fear voiced by Isabella, that foreigners lacked that motivation to defend the interests of the government they served which inspired the native-born. Where armed force was involved there was naturally a more apparent security risk than with civilian officials and the dangers of attracting bellicose foreigners into a country was a theme elaborated by Seyssel.[56] So when Gonzalo de Cordoba asserted that no better militia could be used than that made up of one's own subjects the Great Captain was merely reflecting the fears voiced by Seyssel and Machiavelli concerning the unreliability of foreign mercenaries rather than giving vent to an outburst of national feeling.[57] Yet both Seyssel and Machiavelli linked their discussion closely with the prince's role as commander-in-chief and indeed Machiavelli's own example of the kingdom of France demonstrates not only the importance of the royal initiative but equally the uncertain future of a native force. In none of these areas is there to be found the highly self-conscious, messianic concept of latter-day nationalism.

3

THE REALITY OF POWER

At this stage the point needs to be made that the political development of European countries was neither identical nor simultaneous. The element of force implicit in domestic politics as well as in international rivalries made a greater impression on some countries than on others. Those with a long history of legitimate government, firmly hedged about by subjects' rights and liberties, were less vulnerable than states whose rulers still keenly felt the need to proclaim the authenticity of their rule or who were not restrained by countervailing institutions. In fact, therefore, though all Renaissance rulers adorned themselves like birds of paradise to warn assertive neighbours against invading their ground, not all of them needed to take such measures to reinforce their authority at home.

Francis I cut as magnificent a figure as Henry VIII at the Field of the Cloth of Gold but he depended less than his English cousin upon such display. He was heir to centuries of legitimate kingship handed down from Capetian to Valois according to a fundamental law of succession in favour of the eldest male relative in the direct line of descent, a law that had not been transgressed since Hugh Capet's accession in 987. The French king, therefore, was veritably nominated by the law and by that fact became the pivot not only of the judicial system but of the political order as well. He represented the unity of the state, its integrity and its justice. He was the natural guarantor of the rule of law and the custodian of all those rights and immunities which clergy, noblemen, *bourgeois,* municipal officers and provincial estates, royal officials and the rest had variously acquired. He was also the chief administrator of the kingdom which meant simply that he judged matters of state as matters of law. Francis I's coronation oath, by which he promised to forbid rapacity and injustice and to ordain that all judgments should be based on standards of equity and clemency 'so that a merciful and compassionate God may bestow his clemency upon me',[1] illustrates the official, legalistic view of the prince's public responsibilities. Even matters of foreign policy had to be 'judged' by the magistrate-king. It was no longer possible of course for the king to exercise all his judicial functions in person — he delegated a part of his power to the various supreme courts with their infrastructure of subordinate tribunals. Yet he continued to evoke particularly disputatious or delicate matters to his own royal court where, surrounded by skilled legal advisors — the *maîtres des requêtes* whose service as royal counsellors had begun several centuries before Francis I's accession — he reasserted his direct authority as judge. It was similarly restored, though fleetingly, when he attended those ceremonial sessions of his *parlements* known as *lits de justice*.

These examples do indicate how the king's authority in an increasingly complex situation was constantly in need of adaptation and it is to this element of movement, of change, that we should pay particular attention. Not that French kings had ever dropped or even modified their claim to represent the chief source of judicial authority in the kingdom; but that proud assertion was much closer to being realised in the fifteenth and early sixteenth centuries than it had been, say, some three hundred years earlier, in the days of Saint Louis. In his ordinance of Montils-les-Tours (1454) Charles VII decreed that the diverse legal customs of the kingdom should be set down in writing and after royal confirmation should become the definitive law of the particular region from which they were drawn. This process, which reached its peak during the reigns of Louis XII and Francis I, safeguarded the judicial traditions of the localities but also strengthened the king's supervisory role at the centre. The same comment may be made about the establishment of a number of provincial *parlements* to supplement the activities of the *parlement* of Paris: between 1443 and 1553 seven of these supreme courts were set up at Toulouse, Grenoble, Bordeaux, Dijon, Rouen, Aix-en-Provence and Rennes to dispense royal justice in accordance with the strong local traditions in each of these areas.[2] During the same period the king's justice was ousting a hitherto perfectly acceptable form of customary law, seignorial jurisdiction.[3] This was being effected in a variety of ways: by increasing the number of *cas royaux,* offences like *lèse-majesté* and the waging of private wars which had to be brought before a royal tribunal in the first instance, wherever they were originally committed, by invoking the principle of the appeal from a seignorial to a royal court, and through the theory of *prévention,* whereby royal lawyers maintained that since seignorial justice could be no more than a delegation of the king's justice, his officers were entitled to intervene if cases were not dealt with expeditiously. There were changes taking place too in the relationship between royal and ecclesiastical jurisdictions with the advantage again moving towards the king's judges as they gradually added to the number of offences not covered by privilege of clergy. Finally, at the end of the fifteenth century the introduction of the appeal *comme d'abus* crowned the efforts of the royal courts in this area. By this device the *parlement* of Paris acquired the right to arbitrate between lay and spiritual juris-dictions so that in effect the church could no longer dispute the ultimate judicial supremacy of the king in France. An indication of the monarchs' mounting confidence in their unchallengeable legal status may be gleaned from the great series of royal ordin-ances in which they regulated and defined the manner in which royal justice should be exercised, Montils-les-Tours (1454), Blois (1499), Villers-Cotterets (1539), Moulins (1566).

These developments were all defensible in terms of the king's historic role and of his desire both to expedite justice and respect the multiform judicial traditions of his kingdom, and they all reflected and contributed to the crown's increasing authority.

That authority as we have seen was of one kind and indivisible, so that the prestige gained in the successful pursuit of the most legalistic formulae was also acquired by the ruler in his political role. And there are signs that French kings, bolstered by this swelling authority, were beginning to take political decisions which did not accord with their responsibility as sovereign magistrates. In particular we should observe the long wrangle over the Gallican Liberties, following the publication of the Pragmatic Sanction in 1438.

The Pragmatic Sanction of Bourges represented the essence of traditional Gallican teaching on the authority of ecumenical councils *vis-à-vis* the papacy, on the manner of appointing to benefices in France, on the Pope's claim to tax the French clergy, and was generally considered to comply with the requirements of French custom and canon law. The *parlement* of Paris had no objection to registering it in July 1439, since it conformed admirably with the court's jurisprudential record, which was also the king's. However, shortly after his accession in 1461 Louis XI abrogated the Pragmatic Sanction with a view to strengthening his hold over the French church and eleven years later concluded a concordat with the Pope whose terms included the total abandonment of the Pragmatic Sanction. Following Louis' death the legal situation became obscure, as royal policy towards the Holy See vacillated between apparent acceptance and rejection of the concordat until a new arrangement was negotiated in 1516 between king and Pope — the Concordat of Bologna. Once more the Pragmatic Sanction was revoked and its traditional Gallican principles declared invalid.

In this whole affair the role played by the *parlement* of Paris is instructive.[4] It steadfastly opposed the abolition of the Pragmatic Sanction on the grounds that that act, and not the later concordats, truly represented that Gallican tradition, enshrined in its registers, which could only be overturned at the risk of undermining the king's judicial authority. The magistrates informed Francis I that they considered his concordat to be against the honour of God, the liberties of the Church, the honour of the king and the well-being of his kingdom. After submitting to royal pressure in registering the agreement they drew up a protest indicating that registration had not been by the free will of the *parlement* and that the court would continue to pronounce its judgments according to the terms of the Pragmatic Sanction, and a whole series of *parlementaire* decrees subsequently testified to the magistrates' firmness of purpose. They had acted similarly under Charles VIII and Louis XII whose implicit rejection of the Pragmatic Sanction had not dissuaded the *parlement* from judging cases involving relations between the French church and the papacy in conformity with the dictates of the Pragmatic Sanction.

This resolution on the part of the king's supreme court was not matched by the crown's arbitrary behaviour. The Pragmatic Sanction was published with due ceremony and without recourse to political pressure of any kind after the king had received the weightiest legal advice and following widespread consultation with leading lay and clerical counsellors. Louis XI's abrogation of the act, on the contrary, was by means of simple letters emanating from his council which were not disclosed to the *parlement* at all. His subsequent behaviour in this matter reveals nothing less than contempt for his judicial obligations combined with a shrewd awareness of possible political advantages. By alternately reviving and suspending the Pragmatic Sanction, on each occasion in an unceremonious and informal manner, he sought to win the Pope's support for his Italian policy. Francis I did seek a more traditional and public endorsement of his concordat by registration in the *parlement,* but his methods of obtaining this support were questionable. First, he threatened the magistrates in general terms; then he tried intimidation by sending his uncle, René of Savoy, to observe the court's debates; next, he threatened to replace recalcitrant magistrates and finally he even appeared ready to abolish the stubborn court and convene a new *parlement* at Orléans. His policy of rapprochement with the papacy, like that of Louis XI, was based to some extent upon the assumption that it would strengthen his authority over the church in France but far more upon the hope that it would assist towards the realisation of his Italian ambitions. After the battle of Marignano had given Francis control of Milan he was anxious to press his claim to Naples. To have any hope of success, however, he needed the support of the Pope, who controlled the overland route and was suzerain of the Neapolitan kingdom — hence his readiness to come to terms at Bologna.[5]

What we are observing in this vacillating relationship between the crown and the papacy, and in the consequent dispute between the French kings and their chief court, is the introduction of a new element into the idea of royal justice. While the royal judges delegated to enforce the king's law pursued a policy of respect for legal precedent and proper procedures, in that area where the king had not chosen to delegate his powers, the political arena, he exercised his 'political justice' which was geared not to the judicial principles of the kingdom upheld by the *parlement* but to reasons of state. Thus when the *parlement* tried to scrutinise the wide powers allowed by Francis to the papal legate, the king intervened, remarking that there were good reasons for pleasing the Pope in order that matters of far greater importance, which could not be universally revealed, might be brought to a successful conclusion. No sooner had Francis I succeeded in pushing through the Concordat of Bologna than he began to ignore some of its terms in order to give preferment to loyal and trusted servants whose devotion to the crown was more apparent than their high moral and intellectual qualities.[6]

The French king was also a warrior and Francis I's recent predecessors had finally broken the English grip on France, a triumphant validation of their primary task to defend and maintain their inheritance. But their victory was not achieved without initiating a new relationship between ruler and ruled. A supreme military effort was required to defeat the English and that in turn called for financial resources far beyond the prince's normal reach. Neither the yield from the royal domain, the king's own family estates, nor even the extraordinary grants upon which he had increasingly to rely, sufficed, so that after 1451, with the agreement of certain local estates, the king began to raise money to support his army without their prior approval. As a result, in areas of central France, provincial assemblies disappeared altogether. Similarly, the clergy's financial relationship with the king began to change as the latter shifted the emphasis from direct negotiation with the papacy to the exaction of revenue directly from the French clergy in the form of 'dons gratuits'. This form of taxation was regularised by the Contract of Poissy of 1561 whereby the clergy agreed to pay an annual sum for six years and a smaller grant over the succeeding ten; in fact these subsidies became permanent and tended to grow with increasing royal indigence. As for the towns, in 1515 Francis I created the office of *contrôleur des deniers communs* to exercise a supervisory role over municipal finances; in this area too the crown extended its authority in the course of the sixteenth century.

In all these developments there was an element of force but the pressure was as much on the king to maintain an adequate military machine — as the new threat of Habsburg encirclement promised a danger equal to that so recently overcome — as upon the subjects to provide the necessary funds. So long as the peril was real, and the king was not seeking private profit, then it was felt that he had a right to demand sacrifices from his subjects. Yet in making these demands he was already abdicating his traditional passive role, his uncommitted authority as arbiter, and in established patrimonial terms his subjects could not be blamed for opposing such an extension of princely power. In so far as they did not do so they were conniving with the ruler in redefining the basis of his authority. As the battle between states grew fiercer the French king, like his royal contemporaries in Europe, was coming to expect from his subjects a closer identification with his own personal aspirations, with a greater control over the country's resources and over private individuals than had previously been contemplated, and with a greater emphasis upon the ruler's needs than upon the subjects' rights.[7] Such an increase in power could only be justified in terms of the public good and in France the distinction between the ruler's public and private capacities duly disappeared. Noteworthy therefore was the French king's decision in 1523 to establish a new central treasury, the *trésor de l'Epargne,* into which all his revenues were to be paid, whatever their origin, thus challenging the traditional distinction between extraordinary dues and the resources emanating from the royal domain. Twenty years later Francis I set up sixteen *généralités*, financial and administrative units dividing the country, in each of which a *receveur-général* was appointed to collect all royal revenues without distinction. Other officials were added and from 1577 a new supervisory financial body, the *bureau des finances*, made its appearance in each *généralité*.[8]

However, the dominance achieved by the prince in his public capacity brought its own risks for his subjects: for though they might hope for a community of interest to be formed between ruler and ruled as a result of their closer involvement in public affairs, they had also to fear the encroachment of despotism. The public good might well mean private depradation, particularly under determined and self-willed rulers like Louis XI and Francis I. Once more it was the *parlement* that intervened time and again to remind the ruler of older obligations than that of state interest. Sometimes it was successful, as in 1540, when its objections to a financial edict were accepted by the crown and the legislation was virtually rewritten; sometimes it failed, as in its numerous attempts to prevent the king from selling parts of the royal domain in defiance of a long-held fundamental law of the kingdom. But it is significant that despite periodic royal excursions into arbitrariness under the banner of *raison d'état,* the *parlement's* persistence in reminding the king of his legally based obligations forced him, from time to time, to acknowledge the justice of its opposition and prevented him from rejecting his traditional role altogether.[9]

In the Iberian peninsula we may expect to find a pattern not dissimilar from the French. Ferdinand and Isabella followed the example first set by their twelfth century predecessors in Aragon and Castile, Pedro IV and Fernando III, of bringing security to their lands by the firm establishment of royal judicial authority, though some looked much farther back and imagined they saw in Isabella's royal line the direct descent from Alaric, the Ostrogothic conqueror of Rome.[10] At all events the Catholic kings, in seeking to define their pre-eminence in terms of the power to make and revise laws, had a weighty tradition to support them. They gave substance to their claim by recruiting a lawyer, Montalvo, to compile a volume of 'Royal Ordinances of Castile', published in 1484. This compilation begins, characteristically, with the assertion that 'the true office of the sovereigns is to do judgment and justice'.[11] Yet these ordinances were not intended to override existing rights: respect for the law, natural and divine, permeates the testament of Isabella of Castile, and both she and her husband knew that failure to recognise and defend the rights of their respective subjects would endanger the fragile union of the crowns, the union of two royal houses. Charles V would not change this emphasis and at the end of the sixteenth century the Spanish Jesuit Mariana had the same idea in mind when he wrote that the king had no rights over private possessions but had obligations to maintain internal peace and lead in war.[12] Historians have found no cause to disagree with the contemporary view; in the words of one recent commentator:

Ferdinand and Isabella believed in royal justice, in good kingship. . . . If they had a high sense of their own rights, they also had a high sense of their own obligations, and these included the obligation to respect the right of others. Their divinely appointed task was to restore order and good governance, re-establishing by the exercise of their monarchical power, a society in which each could freely enjoy the rights that belonged to him by virtue of his station.[13]

Mariana reminds us of the king's obligation to lead in war. No Christian prince was under greater pressure to undertake that responsibility than the rulers of Castile and Aragon who were the inheritors of the policy of *reconquista,* the long crusade against the Moorish invaders which, with the conquest of Granada in 1492 and the seizure of Navarre in 1512, merged with the Renaissance battle for security. Ferdinand was faced with the double imbroglio of a holy war against the infidel and a struggle in Italy with the 'French Saracen', Louis XII. Each venture offered a legitimate means of securing the country against an evident danger and there were substantial political prizes to be gathered from the successful pursuit of either course of action. There was one snag, however: a crusade against Islam was an enterprise for all Christendom and surely deserved the support of all Christian princes, something that the French were unwilling to provide. Nevertheless, in pursuing the policy of *reconquista,* Ferdinand also adopted this crusading ideal for it offered the best hope of leaving him free to prosecute his holy war to the utmost benefit to himself, 'joining Heaven and earth, and always to his own advantage'.[14] Thus he preached a moderate division of spoils in Italy and twice arranged two-year truces with France in the hope of finding the way to a definitive peace. Nor should we be entirely cynical about Ferdinand's motives. No Catholic king could easily resist the traditional challenge and Ferdinand's own resolution was stiffened by the promptings of his zealous and strong-willed queen, Isabella. Yet his policy was essentially one of political opportunism, and when Louis XII attacked the papal states in 1511 Ferdinand was not slow to reverse his priorities by deferring his attack on Tunis and joining the Pope and Venice in a Holy League to drive the French out of Italy. Even at this juncture Ferdinand was again able to proclaim that his policy was being shaped by his obligation to defend the church and this was not the last time in sixteenth-century Spain that political interests would fall neatly into the pattern of current orthodoxy. However, in observing the policies of this shrewd and practised politician we can be in no doubt that in the cut-throat world in which he operated traditional and clear-cut military obligations were being obscured by the overriding need to exert some weight on the fluctuating balance of power.

In the Spanish kingdoms, as in France, the growing prestige of the rulers and their urgent financial and military needs enabled the Catholic Kings and their successors, Charles V and Philip II, to extend their authority to a new level. Matching the French king's absorption into his domain of the last feudal stronghold within the kingdom, the Bourbon lands in Auvergne and the Bourbonnais, they too swallowed up wealthy, independent apanages by securing control of the three great Castilian military-religious orders of Santiago, Calatrava and Alcantara, thereby enormously extending their authority, power of patronage, landholding and revenues. They overcame the independence of the Castilian towns by appointing *corregidores,* royal officials with extensive judicial and administrative powers, and bullied the Castilian *cortes* into converting their emergency grants, the *servicios,* into permanent subsidies. They stabilised their income from the Church by changing two provisional contributions, the *tercios reales,* a third of the tithes paid in Castile, and the *cruzada,* into permanent exactions. In fact the rulers of Spain enjoyed an unique financial advantage over their rivals. With the influx of American gold and silver they were able to adopt an independent line where otherwise they would have had to seek supplies with cap in hand. For this reason the *cortes* of Castile suffered an abrupt decline during the reign of Charles V.[15]

They had also to grapple with an unique problem, that of ruling over an Empire which stretched in time across the peninsula to Portugal, east to Italy, north to the Netherlands and west to the Americas. They sought a conciliar solution to this problem, successively establishing councils for Castile (1480) and Aragon (1494), the Indies (1524), Italy (1555-8), Portugal (1580) and Flanders (1588). Thus they presided over the birth of a bureaucratic organisation. A multitudinous hierarchy of royal officials came to serve the king and sometimes, even under the iron regime of the meticulous Philip II, the most influential among them became the effective decision-makers.[16] Philip's father, Charles V, had already decided in 1545 to establish a central archive depository at Simancas to cope with the documentation engendered by this swelling administrative army. By the seventeenth century, political commentators like Saavedra and Quevedo were seriously alarmed. The former remarked in 1640 that 'Authority is lost when the totality of affairs is not in the hands of a single person', and about the same time the latter observed, 'The king who sleeps does not reign . . . and the minister who allows the king to sleep, far from serving him promotes his undoing'.[17] The emerging bureaucracy appeared to pose a threat to the concept of patrimonial government which risked being undermined if the king was removed from the centre of affairs. It might appear in fact that the menacing implication behind the growth of bureaucratic government, that of impersonal unaccountability, was a necessary stage in the development of the idea of the impersonal state. That was not however the case in the Spanish Empire. There the multiplicity of interests militated against the fusion of the ruler's private and public roles since actions taken by him in the public interest as, for example, king of Castile, might well appear as mere private excesses to his subjects in Italy or the Netherlands. There could be no agreed public interest therefore to justify acts that were otherwise unjustifiable. Even less readily than in France could traditional liberties be overridden in favour of a central authority whether bureaucratically organised or not. In fact the Spanish example, where bureaucratic methods were prominent at an early date, suggests that though such methods appear to offer a natural support for the modern impersonal state, they are not necessarily of great significance in inspiring the idea. Support for this conclusion may be found in the Russian experience where, despite the emergence of the impersonal state-idea at a relatively early date under Peter the Great, there was no bureaucracy worth talking about in the seventeenth and early eighteenth centuries. Peter's attempts at establishing a centralised administrative system, though a degree more sophisticated than the *prikazy* structure which he sought to replace, was inefficient and of little relevance to the evolution of the state-idea elaborated by the tsar. In Brandenburg-Prussia, on the other hand, the Great Elector's establishment of an ever larger permanent army and of a centralising bureaucratic structure based on the *Generalkriegskommissariat* did contribute to the emergence of the concept of an impersonal state under his great-grandson, Frederick the Great.[18]

On both sides of the Pyrenees in the sixteenth century the continuing vigour of ancient rights may be observed. On the Spanish side they were inherited through the crown of Aragon and asserted in a proud and independent spirit, best captured in the famous apocryphal oath of the Aragonese to their king: 'We, who are worth as much as you, make you our king and lord provided that you guard for us our *fueros* and liberties, and if not, not.'[19] This form of words, evolved between 1550 and 1565 when disagreement between the Aragonese and their ruler

Philip II was becoming acute, epitomises an attitude which Philip himself was prepared to countenance, for after subduing the revolt of Aragon in 1591 he at once confirmed almost all its privileges. The far more serious rebellion in Catalonia in 1640 ended in a similar way with Philip IV's promise to maintain that principality's laws and liberties in their traditional form. Indeed, the period from the fall of Olivares to the end of Habsburg rule in Spain has been called 'an age of almost superstitious respect for regional rights and privileges by a Court too weak and too timid to protest'.[20]

In Russia on the other hand the achievements of able and ambitious rulers pushed that country closer to the Leviathan. In the latter part of the fifteenth century an internecine struggle, reminiscent of the Italian wars of the early *quattrocento,* was taking place in the Russian lands as the grand duke of Muscovy sought to confirm the primacy of his state in the Russian world and to break the landholding independence of his own great subjects. Ivan III succeeded in absorbing the apanage principalities and initiated the long process, culminating in a savage administrative reorganisation (the *oprichnina* of his grandson, Ivan the Terrible) whereby the Muscovite land was converted from hereditary to service tenure. By the time of the first Romanov's accession in 1613, most land was *pomestie,* bestowed by the tsar in return for military or administrative service, and most noblemen were *pomeshchiki,* service gentry who needed the prince's support in a way that their *boyar* predecessors had never done. As a result, the dangerously fissile tendency of the Muscovite state was arrested; the country was pulled together by the unifying influence of the house of Rurik.

Initially the grand duke's authority was patrimonial as it was in the west — Moscow belongs to Ivan III, noted Contarini.[21] Indeed justification for the *pomestie* system grew out of the concept of the Muscovite land as the ruler's personal estate from whom it might be leased, but never bought. But the country's political and social structure very quickly pressed the tsars towards a view of government different from that of the traditionally-based monarchies of France and Spain. Muscovite society was organised on a military basis to fight enemies like Novgorod and Pskov in the Russian world, and Sweden, the Livonian knights and the arch-foe, Poland-Lithuania, further afield. The tsars had to be able to raise and maintain an army and they employed the *pomestie* system to guarantee the permanent availability of a native-Russian force. These part-time knights were not the only social group affected by government demands. To ensure that land remained under cultivation during prolonged absences on military service the gentry required a permanent labour force which would also provide them with regular and much needed dues. Otherwise their estates would not provide an adequate basis for the necessary service and failure to perform that service could lead to land deprivation: hence the pressure for the extension of bondage. For a variety of reasons the government was prepared to support this demand. If the gentry's estates went to rack and ruin their vital military capacity would be seriously impaired. Besides, it was convenient for the tsar to know the whereabouts of peasant farmers for purposes of taxation, and from the sixteenth century he employed his part-time soldiers as part-time tax collectors too.[22] In fact the need to raise revenue from a disconcertingly mobile population, about whom the government had practically no reliable information, persuaded the tsar of the advantage of pinning to the spot, in this way, all his taxable subjects: thus farmers on state lands and merchants in towns also found their lives drastically circumscribed as a result of the government's financial stringency.

In enforcing this policy the tsar was supported by a tradition of service to authority which the Mongol conquerors of the Golden Horde had first established during their period of domination, and by his alliance with the orthodox church which offers an unique example of *rapport* between the secular and spiritual powers. This course of action reached a climax in 1649 when Tsar Alexis's law code gave legal sanction to serfdom. By then every individual in the state had acquired a primary obligation to serve, and nobody had the right to put his personal interests or inclinations first. Nobody, that is, except the tsar. For what had been effected in Muscovy at an early stage was the total union of the ruler's public and private roles. There, there were no political institutions strong enough to challenge the tsardom: even the *zemsky sobor,* which was responsible for the election of two tsars, Boris Godunov and Michael Romanov, remained through most of its brief and discontinuous history the ruler's creature.[23] Nor, more significantly, were there any legal traditions capable of sheltering the subject from direct tsarist control, however arbitrary that might prove to be. The concept of positive law was not to be found in Muscovy. The tsar was not seen as a legislator and judge as he was in some western European countries, though he did settle individual cases brought before him and from time to time he did promulgate codes of law. But these were all *ad hoc* solutions to particular problems. The tradition of the saint-prince inherited by the Romanov house from a line of canonised rulers offers a clue to the concept of justice appertaining in Russia: the tsar's personal piety was considered adequate to guarantee that the regime of Divine Justice would operate in Muscovy.[24] The idea offered in theory a splendid vision of Utopia, though in practice it only guaranteed the legal supremacy of the tsar. In the absence of these balancing factors the tsar's private interests became effectively those of the state. This sort of identification produced a political organisation thoroughly committed to the ruler's interests and a public morality not readily justified even according to the erastian tenets of the Russian orthodox church.

It was a situation achieved by force—directly, culminating in the *oprichnina* and the sack of Novgorod in 1570, and indirectly, through the government's support for the system of personal bondage. It was this characteristic of *force majeure* which persuaded western critics like Bishop Bossuet that the tsar of Muscovy was a despot. However, he was making that judgment in the context of Louis XIV's France, where the idea of dynastic, personal kingship had not yet been effectively challenged. In Russia, on the other hand, change had been far more rapid and though Ivan the Great has been compared with his fifteenth-century French contemporary, Louis XI,[25] a similar comparison in the seventeenth century would be meaningless. The relationship

of the tsar's subjects to their ruler in the years immediately prior
to the accession of Peter I (1689) was one of such total obligation
that it could not be adequately expressed even in terms of
personal despotism. A different rationale was emerging: especially
after the Time of Troubles (1584–1613) when Muscovy survived
the threat of Polish and Swedish annexation without an acceptable ruling dynasty, an idea of the impersonal state as the source
and justification of the subjects' absolute dependence began to
take root and would be clearly enunciated by Peter the Great.[26]
The pressures of war and the absence of a legal framework for
political action, these were the key factors in the Russian situation.

So it was with Brandenburg-Prussia. The fear of external
aggression was the key to Frederick William's campaign against
the Estates. The pattern of a strong ruler whose achievements,
especially his flouting of inherited conventions, pushed him
imperceptibly towards a new state concept was broadly comparable with the Russian example. The scattered nature of the
Great Elector's inheritance explains the belated emergence of
Brandenburg-Prussia, so that when this powerful and effective
ruler made his impact it was in the environment of mid-
seventeenth century Europe. Thereupon the changes which he
inaugurated proceeded much more quickly than would have
been possible a century earlier. His great-grandson, Frederick II,
thus became the first European ruler, after Peter the Great, to
make explicit his belief in the idea of service by the sovereign as
well as by his subjects to the impersonal state.[27]

Developments in England put that country somewhere between
the French and Spanish models on the one hand and the Russian
on the other. The Tudors succeeded in establishing a moderately
firm grip on their realm. In achieving their objective the dynasty
acted ruthlessly when it had to, capriciously on occasion, but
by choice within the framework of the common law. Like their
French counterparts the Tudors inherited a traditional respect
for advice and a chronically depleted treasury. In attempting to
remedy the latter they were slow to fall back on extraordinary
grants, preferring to increase the efficiency of their financial
administration in order to exact all that was due to them. As a

result they succeeded — or more accurately Henry VIII's great
minister, Thomas Cromwell, succeeded — in creating a central-
government machine which both improved the revenue yield
and, in the shape of the privy council, made available to the ruler
permanent official advice. These developments of the 1530s have
been described as inaugurating national and bureaucratic methods
of government, 'divorced from service on the king's person and
endowed with a lasting independence from the whim of the
moment or the influence of individuals'.[28] Having in mind the
examples of France and especially Spain, we must be chary of
attributing a teleological progression to such developments,
though in England, as elsewhere, it was undoubtedly the case
that the dynasty's success in confirming its authority was steadily
undermining the very idea of dynastic rule. Yet the speed at
which this process took place should not be exaggerated. Government continued to depend very heavily upon the ruler's personality and, even during the reign of Charles I, royal officials were
still accustomed to look upon themselves as private, not public
servants.[29] However, the rate of change was faster than in France
or Spain, for, like the grand dukes of Muscovy, the Tudors'
chief claim to rule was that they were effectively doing so
already. Therefore they did not automatically inherit, as an
essential aspect of their kingship, the obligation to respect and
maintain ancient liberties, a duty which continued to inhibit
European princes of more distinguished pedigree. Consequently,
again like the house of Rurik, they were able to require a degree
of submission from their subjects which went beyond personal
despotism.

The key issue, however, in the evolution of the English political
structure was the religious revolution of the sixteenth century.
The Reformation was of course an important element in the
whole matter under discussion but nowhere was it more pertinent
than in England where parliamentary statute was the crucial
instrument. In effecting his religious revolution, Henry VIII
established not a Tudor despotism but the incipient despotism of
the state. Through parliament the king took over the headship

of the Church, together with the authority to appoint its chief
dignitaries, to tax and administer it, and to provide the final
court of appeal for the clergy; and his daughter, embracing the
German solution of *cuius regio eius religio*, effectively prescribed
the form of her subjects' religion. This unheard-of extension of
royal power was carried through with parliamentary support
so that its architects, by invoking an ill-defined 'body politic'
might hope to justify what had hitherto been unjustifiable. They
succeeded so well that henceforth nothing ordained by parliamentary decree would require further justification: 'The voice
of parliament had become the voice of God.'[30]

Henry VIII might have maintained that the need for security
properly justified his actions and that his methods bore the stamp
of legality that was needed for him to play his traditional part in
defending his subjects' rights. But no dispassionate observer
could ignore the massive consolidation of princely power taking
place behind the guileful façade nor the element of force, more
sophisticated, less apparent and more effective than in Muscovy,
by which the king bent his subjects' loyalty to a new credo.
Though Machiavelli observed, in his cynical way, that a man
would more quickly forget the execution of his father than the
violation of his property, Henry's treason laws contemplated a
far more cynical violation than the Italian ever alleged — that of
his subjects' innermost thoughts.[31] No patrimonial ruler could
ever make such demands; yet for some time incantatory allusions
to the 'body politic' and the 'common weale' effectively disguised the masterly Tudor legerdemain. However, despite the
royal ascendancy, the situation in England following the political
reformation of the 1530s was one of fundamental instability since
a patrimonial monarchy was attempting to shoulder a weight of
authority which could not be justified in terms of traditional
dynasticism. There would have to be adaptation and change or
princely power would risk total collapse.

In Sweden the newly established Vasa ruler, viewed as an
usurper by most foreign princes and at odds with the Pope, also
cast envious eyes upon the economic resources of the Church.
No doubt mindful of his chancellor's observation that the

church's wealth properly belonged to the whole community of the faithful, Gustav Vasa, like his Tudor contemporary, Henry VIII, decided to associate the body politic with his revolution. In 1527 in the Västerås Recess the three estates of the *Riksdag* gave the king the lead he wanted and in the following years he plundered the church's wealth relentlessly. The final royal *coup* came in 1539 when Gustav promulgated a regulation for the government of the church, effectively translating it into a bureaucratic department, controlled by the secular power which claimed the right to regulate every aspect of church life. And not only church life; in a letter contemporary with the regulation the king admonished his subjects to be 'attentive and obedient to our royal command both in wordly things, as also in religious; and you shall do only that which we prescribe to you by our royal mandate, both in matter spiritual, and in matters lay'.[32] In fact, Gustav's success in first stabilising the new regime and then extending royal authority was, by this time, having familiar visible effects.

The clear comparison with England may be extended further into the field of government administration where Swedish efforts reflected, if they did not quite match, the work of Thomas Cromwell. When the Vasa line acquired the Swedish throne in 1523 the royal administration was 'scarcely more than estate management raised to a higher power'.[33] By 1540, however, a still rudimentary conciliar system with a corresponding provincial organisation had been born, professionally administered and reflecting the rapid expansion of the area of government activity. As in England, the change was not effected overnight. Indeed, the initial bureaucratic experiments for the most part did not survive Gustav's own reign and it was not until the reign of his great successor, Gustav Adolph (1611–32) that an effective administrative regime was firmly established. We have already observed that the emergence of bureaucratic procedures offers but fallible guidance in tracing the state's evolution and that fact must be borne in mind in considering the Swedish model. Nevertheless, there do appear to be some indications to suggest that the concept of an omnicompetent authority taking over from that of a family business made steadier progress in Sweden than in England. This is to allege neither that the Vasas were less dynastically inclined than the Tudors — Gustav schemed for twenty years to establish his family as the hereditary royal house — nor that the idea of an impersonal state was close to formulation in sixteenth-century Sweden. But Sweden was a brand-new patrimony owing its independent existence to its Vasa rulers and subjected to fierce external pressures. Its situation, in other words, was much more comparable with that of Muscovy than with England. As in Muscovy the opportunity existed for the ruler to identify public interest exclusively with his own so that the exercise of what, in other situations, would appear to be characteristically patrimonial authority at once threatened to become something rather different. This may be seen in Gustav Vasa's view of landholding, which by 1539 was apparently that all land belonged to the crown and those non-nobles enjoying temporary possession of it could only expect continued tenure while they fulfilled their fiscal obligations to the government. The idea was further developed by Charles IX at the beginning of the seventeenth century into the concept of aristocratic service to the state, which frequently involved the gift of land in hereditary tenure conditional upon the performance of military or administrative service. This was a development very reminiscent of the *pomestie* system which operated in Muscovy. Gustav's decision in 1544 to establish the first permanent native force in Europe, by conscripting one peasant in every ten (one in twenty of the nobles' peasants) into the Swedish army also merits attention. Here he anticipated Peter the Great's military reforms, after the disastrous Russian defeat by the Swedes at Narva, by establishing a royal army whose *raison d'être* went far beyond mere loyalty to the ruling house. In all this, the Reformation played a notable part for, whereas in England, it only quickened and accentuated current trends, in Sweden it crucially affected the formative years of the new state.

In neighbouring Denmark the influence of the Reformation was similarly deeply felt. After Frederick I's death in 1533 a disputed succession brought the country close to dissolution until

Christian III achieved power in 1536. His victory, like that of
Gustav Vasa, was enough in itself to give him a surfeit of
authority and he moved against the church whose financial
resources he desperately needed to usurp. In so doing he further
consolidated his own position and significantly extended the area
of government intervention. Following a session of the *Rigsdag,*
convened in October 1536, the power of the bishops was overthrown and with it that of the old church, the totality of civil and
ecclesiastical power being invested in the king and his council.
Episcopal property became royal, episcopal tithes went, likewise,
to the crown for the establishment of schools and the support of
learned men, and a third of all remaining tithes were also allocated
to the crown for the maintenance of scholars. Additionally it was
decreed that hospitals should be adequately equipped by the
central authority and in every town 'respectable and prudent'
men were appointed to look after the sick and unemployed;
though, on the other side, begging by the able-bodied was
declared punishable by death.[34] This degree of social organisation and control from the centre is remarkable and comparable
with the administration and enforcement of the Poor Law in
Elizabethan England, where the most effective comprehensive
system of poor relief was evolved.[35]

There was no Reformation on the western model in Muscovy,
but there was a shift in relations between the secular and spiritual
powers which had a more spectacular effect there than anywhere
else on the emergence of the modern state. Since the Russian
conversion to Byzantine orthodoxy in the eleventh century the
church had played a significant, but increasingly obscurantist,
political role. The alliance struck between the Russian Orthodox
Church, which considered itself to be the sole legitimate re-
pository of Christianity following the apostasy of Rome and
Byzantium, and the secular rulers of Moscow ensured that, by
the seventeenth century, Muscovy was dominated by the theo-
cratic mission of her church and paralysed by this doctrine of the
third Rome, a doctrine emphasising her uniqueness but at the
expense of growing isolation. The tsar was already the head of
the church but shackled by a quasi-spiritual role which dangerous-

ly limited his freedom of action and further heightened his country's vulnerability. Following the reforms of Patriarch Nikon and his subsequent quarrel with the tsar Alexis in the mid-seventeenth century, two episodes which weakened the old order, Peter the Great acted decisively by abolishing the patriarchate and instituting the Holy Synod (1721) to govern the church.[36] The significance of this change went far beyond mere organisational or administrative reform. The church thereby lost its hold over the secular power; henceforth its role would be subordinate and of diminishing significance in comparison with the power of the state. For, having destroyed the ancient foundation of Russian government, Peter was forced to invoke a new ideology to take its place, and for the first time in Europe, clearly and unequivocally, the idea of the impersonal, all-powerful State was proclaimed, a startling touch of modernity from an unexpected quarter. From his reign come legislative references to 'interest of state'; the stipulation that his subjects should take two oaths of loyalty, to the monarch and to the state; the institution of a table of ranks, whose object was the recruitment of talented and disinterested rather than privileged officers and bureaucrats; the establishment of a native conscript army. Most remarkable of all was Peter's personal subjugation to the abstraction which he acknowledged as the ultimate and supreme object of service for himself and his people.[37] There are comparisons, therefore, to be drawn between Peter's Reformation and its western archetype, despite substantial differences in chronology and religious background.[38]

This important aspect of the Russian situation needs to be borne in mind along with those significant factors which have already been noted: the threat of external aggression which was the chief dynamic of Peter's reign, and the absence of inherited restraints which, had they existed, might have inhibited the actions of the tsar and autocrat once he had broken out of his spiritual strait-jacket.

Religious revolution was also of profound significance in the Netherlands, though it came not from Wittenberg in the east, but down the Rhine from Geneva. And what a superb instrument,

in Dutch hands, was the doctrine of Calvin, fashioned to with-
stand the opposition of princes as well as their support. Here was
a religion entirely independent in organisation and preaching the
duty of estates to oppose the unjust actions of governments.
Armed with this new creed the Netherlanders succeeded, entirely
against the prevailing European mood, in overthrowing princely
power altogether, 'the first decisive defeat of dynasticism rampant
and the establishment of a middle-class Republic'.[39] It was a
famous victory and deeply significant. Royal government was
replaced by a new political order whose survival would depend
upon the common acceptance not of a family but of a fleetingly
national idea, inchoately and precociously felt, an order which
many contemporaries believed impossible to sustain. The
importance of this development in the history of the modern
state scarcely needs underlining.

In conclusion, several additional observations may be made
upon the religious divisions of Europe. Protestantism failed
especially where dynastic considerations formed part and parcel of
a wider, long-standing *rapport* between ruler and ruled, a fact
which further explains the relatively slow emergence of the idea
of the impersonal state in France, Spain and the Habsburg Empire.
In all these countries the very foundation of government was
bound up with the support and maintenance of the old church
itself and not merely with a general spiritual allegiance, and,
whatever the theological extravagances adopted among some of
their subjects, it was inherently unlikely that their Most Christian
and Catholic Majesties and the Holy Roman Emperor himself
would choose, Samson-like, to bring down the pillars of their own
authority. Yet the Reformation did have a part to play in the
development of the modern state even in those countries where it
failed to take root. They could not ignore the pattern of events in
those parts of Europe that did espouse the new faith and in reacting
to the situation these monarchs too were pushed a little further
towards accepting a novel state-concept. In particular, they were
bound to pursue the policy of *cuius regio eius religio* which both
implied an extension of government power over all the individuals
within the state and brought an added sense of identity and unity

to its corporate membership, the 'body politic'.

These twin developments were more powerfully felt, of course, in those states whose rulers did reject the old faith, partly because there were not the same pressures acting against change and partly because the doctrine of the Reformation, when given its head, was bound to encourage them. Not that the idea of the modern state as an abstract reality governing the life of the people is to be found anywhere in Luther's teaching, it is not; but there is to be found a significant broadening of the area of government intervention, to include responsibility for the physical as well as the moral welfare of the subjects.[40] In the complex, and still only partially explored, area of European poor relief in the early modern period there are dangers in being too dogmatic. Professor Pullan's researches in sixteenth-century Venice have led him to conclude that

> . . . general attitudes to the poor were often determined by a rather similar mixture of pity and fear, of genuine humanity and brutal paternalism, and by a similar determination to eliminate criminals and social parasites — whether a given society had remained Catholic, or whether it had severed its allegiance to Rome.[41]

Yet he also acknowledges the continuing importance of the church's role in Italy, while in Spain the influence of the mendicant orders defied attempts by the secular authorities to intervene in the field of public charity. Similarly, in France as late as the eighteenth century 'The succouring of the poor . . . was not the business of a laicized parish rate, as in England, but was dependent upon the alms of the faithful'.[42] In Protestant countries, on the other hand, monastic charity had come to an end and Luther's solution was to rely upon the secular community as a whole to fill the vacuum. Luther himself wrote that 'the office of the magistrate is to bear the hardships, burdens and quarrels of the people in order that he may acknowledge himself to be their servant, not their master',[43] an observation closer to the eighteenth-century views of Frederick the Great of Prussia than to that of a Renaissance prince. It follows, too, from Luther's teaching, that subjects could not, under any circumstances, rebel against the secular power since that power also represented their own highest spiritual aspirations. Rulers who opted for Reform, therefore, found themselves presiding over regimes self-consciously concerned with the spiritual and political orthodoxy of their subjects and with the corresponding unorthodoxy of their neighbours. There was little room in this situation for the survival unimpaired of traditional princely government. Consequently there was a tendency, already observed in England, for countries adopting Protestantism to evolve new political structures and subsequently to promote new intellectual attitudes towards the state.

Finally, though all governments were adopting an exclusive and intolerant attitude within their own frontiers, relations between states were moving in a strikingly different direction. Examples are numerous: Francis I's diplomatic initiatives at the Porte and in the direction of the German Protestant princes; Elizabeth I's attempt to secure Turkish aid against Spain in the 1580s; Philip II's efforts to prevent the pope from issuing the fateful *Regnans in Excelsis* against the English queen in 1570; Gustav Vasa's flirtation with the Habsburgs in 1540; the Franco-Swedish alliance of 1631; and continuing French support for the Dutch down to the reign of Louis XIV. As religious uniformity became an increasingly important constituent in terms of national security, buttressing the authority of the ruler and at the same time diminishing its personal character, so the latent amorality governing international relations, to which Machiavelli had previously drawn attention, was ironically brought further into the open, for whereas even the most self-willed and unscrupulous prince could not escape the pressure of moral considerations no such limitation marred the pursuit of the disembodied national interest.[44]

4

THE QUEST FOR SOVEREIGNTY (I):
REVOLTS IN FRANCE AND THE LOW COUNTRIES

The expanding power of the prince, in part a concomitant of the religious upheavals outlined in the previous chapter, so transformed the political climate in Europe that already by 1600 it was becoming clear that neither the petty tyrannies of Italy nor the universalist aspirations of Emperor and Pope offered any sort of model or example for contemporary politicians. What the new order was to be, however, remained far from clear. Europe was in a condition of great tension and flux as old answers about the nature and extent of royal authority and the rights and obligations of subjects failed to satisfy new questions about the limits of reason of state, about the public responsibility of governments to command, and the private right of subjects to dissent. The prince himself stood at a crossroads, borne down by an authority too weighty now to be justified in personal or dynastic terms, increasingly vulnerable to domestic resentment and ultimately to rebellion in the absence of some other mutually acceptable justification. For that reason, as princely power stretched subjects' loyalty to breaking point, it may properly be claimed that the political development of Europe reached a crucial stage in the closing decades of the sixteenth century. The first open rifts developed in France with the Wars of Religion and in the Spanish Empire with the Dutch Revolt.

The unexpected death of Henry II in 1559 provided the opportunity for simmering discontent to break out into the open. His successor, Francis II, was only fifteen years old and incapable of exerting the personal authority necessary to deflect the opposition. It was something of a paradox in fact that the antagonism inspired by the Crown's more public, less personal image could only be expressed openly when the ruler himself lacked the strength of personality to enforce his authority. That was because the French monarch, as we have seen, traditionally maintained a formidable hold over his subjects' minds so that when the crisis came, and one youthful and inadequate ruler succeeded another, the issue long remained in doubt and the final resolution incorporated a greater degree of compromise than in those other states which were about to face a similar crisis. The French crown re-established its old authority and went on to develop an even more formidable hold upon the country, but it remained sensitive to that earlier tradition which had inspired the challenge of the near-disastrous Wars of Religion.

The three inter-related elements which provoked that struggle all stemmed, directly or indirectly, from the same root cause: the changing nature of government which no longer seemed willing either to guarantee the *status quo* or to delimit the area of its intervention. First, there was the loss of status affecting powerful, princely and aristocratic families whose former relationship had allowed them direct access to the monarch, but who now found themselves removed, at one step, as legal, financial and administrative experts were summoned increasingly to cope with expanding government business. Already, as in England, the secretaries of state were showing signs of approaching indispensability and the royal council itself was becoming a more complex and professional forum, unsympathetic to the judgment of amateurs, however well-born. This was not an altogether new feature in France and it would be misleading to exaggerate the degree of novelty: but at this time feelings of resentment were reinforced by the growing disparity between the provincial and local influence of these aristocratic families on the one hand, and their declining role at central government level on the other, precisely when the area of central government activity was expanding.[1] They were also reinforced by the other two motives for opposition which were likewise concerned with status and the *status quo*. The first of these motives was economic.

The Italian wars of Francis I and Henry II had been expensive and the burden of the *taille,* a direct tax on persons and, in some cases, on land, crippling on many of the unprivileged class who had to pay it. The ramifications of this fact were felt higher up the social scale, for the impoverished tenants could not pay their feudal dues, and younger sons and lesser noblemen, at least, found it increasingly difficult to swim against the rising tide of prices, particularly since the *seigneur's* authority to raise money from his peasants was another matter falling increasingly under the super-vision of the central government. Additionally, the noble class had made unprecedented financial contributions to the war effort in the shape of forced loans and investments in royal schemes which paid no interest because, by 1557, Henry II was bankrupt. Even the noble stock-in-trade of war was no longer a paying proposition though when it came to an end, with the treaty of Cateau-Cambrésis in 1559, there were many who felt that the last hope of recouping their financial losses had been extinguished. There were others, too, who felt keenly a sense of alienation, artisans and small shopkeepers in the towns, caught in the vice of rising prices and heavy war taxation, and journeymen who had to survive without the assistance of the exclusive guild system.[2]

Such discontent in so many quarters presented a serious enough problem for the youthful Francis II and his mother, Catherine de Medici, but when the third, and much the most significant element, that of religious dissent, was joined to the other two, the French crown was confronted with a veritable crisis of confidence during which its very existence was called into question. After a youthful flirtation with Erasmian unorthodoxy Francis I, and his son, had acted firmly against French Protestantism, a policy more successful against Lutheranism, which required the prince's support, than Calvinism, which did not. And it was Calvinism, spreading like wildfire in the months and years after Henry II's death, that welded the various dissident elements in the state into a highly organised and challenging force. The purposes and motives of its adherents were various — the desire to regain lost power, status and resources mingling with the fervent expectation of a new moral order and of new opportunities for the dispossessed. The political leadership of the movement stood for retrenchment rather than revolution and its spiritual chiefs too sought acceptability rather than converts for their creed. Yet both flew in the face of the reality of the contemporary political situation whereby the crown was justified in overriding private rights in the interests of what it considered to be the public good. In 1559 the public good might certainly be thought to include the preservation of royal authority unimpaired and the principle of *cuius regio eius religio*. Consequently through four reigns and for over thirty years bitter civil wars flared intermittently and ultimately the essentially conservative opposition of the early years came close to provoking a genuine political revolution.

Predictably the strife of the Wars of Religion had a hothouse effect upon political ideas since they raised for the first time, in a manner that could brook no evasion, the significant question of the extent of the government's powers of intervention and coercion and the even more crucial question of the positive political rights of the subject, something which up to this time had not been seen as separate from, much less in opposition to, those of the prince, but always as a reflection of princely power, the natural corollory of his authority. At first the Huguenots maintained the principle of passive obedience which was central to the teaching of Calvin himself, but, especially after the Saint Bartholomew Day Massacre in 1572, it became extremely difficult for French Calvinists to support such a principle. Their alternative programme, though by no means an unambiguous or fully coherent statement, is best summed up in the *Vindiciae Contra Tyrannos* of 1579. Here is to be found a hotch-potch of ideas, not particularly startling or original in themselves, still essentially concerned with the established political order but with a new emphasis that suggested the possibility of a transformation. There was the idea of a federal structure based on the reality of the established Huguenot enclaves, which helps to explain the pamphlet's popularity in the Low Countries; there was the vaguely formulated belief in a contract between king and people which gave the *Vindiciae* such a vogue in seventeenth-century England; and there was an attempt to define the objectives of the community in establishing the political order: defence against external aggression and the administration of justice to the subjects. Amid the contradictions and illogicalities of the argument it is possible to glimpse the shift in the balance between prince and people. The state is not the ruler's patrimony and, though the subjects' role is one of obligation in return for security from outside aggression and a tranquil judicial regime at home, the prince's obligation is unconditional. The community itself established the state for its own good and government exists simply to implement the community's wishes. The subject does not hold privilege and status from the supreme judge so much as he positively requires the executive to protect him and his property.[3]

The change in Huguenot theory did not survive the emergence of the compromise *Politique* movement and the appearance of the Protestant Henry of Navarre as a likely successor to the French throne, and the ideas of the *Vindiciae* were jettisoned in favour of a reaffirmation of the original Calvinist belief in passive obedience. By the 1580s there was, in any case, no lack of ardent advocates of traditional princely authority and from among their ranks came Pierre de Belloy, who in his *Apologie Catholique* of 1585 and the more famous *De l'Autorité du Roi* published two years later, first enunciated the doctrine of divine-right monarchy in France. It was a predictable idea, to boost an ailing power by linking it indissolubly with the Almighty with whom princes had long claimed an intimate relationship, in order to persuade the more sceptical among their subjects of the legitimacy of their rule. Belloy was going much further, of course, by alleging that by virtue of his divine appointment the king could not be opposed in whatever enterprises he chose to undertake.[4] His intention was to justify, not to define, the plenitude of princely power which he believed it would be necessary to invoke if France was to be rescued from civil war. The critical task of definition had already been performed a decade earlier by the most important political writer to emerge during the period of the Wars of Religion, Jean Bodin, whose views deserve particular consideration.

In some ways Bodin's *Six Livres de la République* is a disappointing work, marred by serious inconsistencies even in matters close to the heart of his argument,[5] but unlike the author of the *Vindiciae* he has no illusions about the essential nature of political power and the manner in which it must always be exercised. His *chef d'œuvre*, published in 1576, was, like the *Vindiciae*, written under the stress of the French crisis, and in consequence it too shows signs of a changing emphasis in the relationship between ruler and ruled. Nothing survives in Bodin of the old patrimonial concept. The royal domain, once both the heart of the country and the prince's private estate, is for him the public domain whose revenues are not for the prince to use as he wills, for he is only the administrator, not the owner and, once the normal expenses of the commonwealth have been met, any funds remaining from this source ought to be employed for 'some public necessity'.[6] He also elaborated a more homogenous political order, alleging a greater community of interest between ruler and subject than had been tenable heretofore. 'It must however be emphasized', he wrote, 'that it is not the rights and privileges which he enjoys which makes a man a citizen, but the mutual obligation between subject and sovereign, by which, in return for the faith and obedience rendered to him, the sovereign must do justice and give . . . protection to the subject.'[7] But the crucial element in Bodin's thought is his recognition of the fact that whatever the appearances of mutual obligation, if the political order is to survive, power must in fact rest unchallenged with the sovereign. In other words, the element of force which Machiavelli and some of his contemporaries had earlier observed as a largely subterranean aspect, was now coming to the surface to be recognised as truly the ultimate guarantor of the state's existence. 'Reason and common sense alike point to the conclusion that the origin and foundation of commonwealth was in force and violence', Bodin remarked, and cited the works of Thucydides, Plutarch and Caesar in support of his observation.[8] It was now possible to distinguish such a basis for political authority with certainty precisely because the personal, patrimonial basis of a century before, which could not be divorced entirely from moral considerations, was no longer tenable, whereas the new emphasis upon maintaining the interests of the community as a whole, including the ruler, placed upon the sovereign the chief obligation of maintaining the state's existence, a requirement only tenuously linked with the dictates of private morality.

The sovereign prince, who was also the image of God on earth (a point at which Bodin's argument would shortly be helped out by that of Belloy) should under normal circumstances act as his predecessors had done. Many of Bodin's observations fit perfectly into the pattern of early sixteenth-century monarchy:

The true function of the prince is to judge his people. He must of course also be armed against the enemy, but justice is his necessary attribute in all places, and at all times; [and again] . . . nothing so tends to the preservation of commonwealths as religion, since it is the force that at once secures the authority of kings and governors, the execution of the laws, the obedience of subjects, reverence for the magistrates, fear of ill-doing, and knits each and all in the bonds of friendship;

[or finally:] The surest foundation of a commonwealth is public confidence, for without it neither justice, nor any sort of lasting association is possible. Confidence only arises where promises and legal obligations are honoured. If these obligations are cancelled, contracts annulled, debts abolished, what else can one expect but the total subversion of the state, for none would any longer have any confidence in his fellows. . . .[9]

But times would not always be normal and then the admonitions became very different:

. . . he [the prince] cannot take his subjects' property without just and reasonable cause, that is to say by purchase, exchange, legitimate confiscation, or to secure peace with the enemy when it cannot be otherwise achieved. Natural reason instructs us that the public good must be preferred to the particular, and that subjects should give up not only their mutual antagonisms and animosities, but also their possessions, for the safety of the commonwealth. . . .[10]

Thus extraordinary taxes are always justified in times of crisis, laws may be imposed without the consent of subjects, the powers of magistrates may be revoked by the mere presence of the sovereign. In a memorable phrase Bodin sums up his thesis: 'nothing is more just than that which is necessary'.[11]

When the triumphant Henry IV uttered his much-quoted remark that Paris was worth a mass, he was no doubt unintentionally paraphrasing Bodin for posterity. Certainly that much converted monarch was buoyed up by the support of such ideas that helped to produce a climate of opinion in which most of the dissident elements were content to fall in behind the crown, so that eventually even the genuinely revolutionary threat posed by that faction of the reconstituted Catholic League, which in 1583 had driven his predecessor from his own capital, withered away.[12] The French monarchy survived and prospered in the following century and undoubtedly Bodin and Belloy can claim some share of the credit for that. But if the king of France emerged more self-assured, more god-like than ever, and reason of state became increasingly his government's veritable *lingua franca*, his victory was far from total. The restrictive traditions of the monarchy still inhibited even the most absolute of kings. Nourished by the legalistic stance of the *parlement* of Paris, by the independent spirit of the provinces and of their local estates, even by the unwillingness of the king and his ministers except *in extremis* to challenge established custom, old traditions held out against the new. None of the ministers who were most successful in managing the country's finances — Sully, Richelieu and Colbert in the seventeenth century, Fleury in the eighteenth — did more than make the best of the existing system. French kings were frequently in urgent need of money, even seriously threatened militarily by the lack of it, and Bodin would certainly have approved of Louis XIV's emergency exactions of the *dixième* and the *capitation*. But might he not also have been a little surprised at the quickness with which so authoritarian a sovereign acknowledged the temporary nature of such measures?[13]

In contributing his concept of sovereignty Bodin also gave form to the idea of the state as an intimate union of ruler and ruled, a half-way concept between the patrimonial view of the Renaissance monarchies and that of the abstract entity which could not yet be contemplated. He was also, therefore, the first modern political theorist to uncover if not fully to comprehend that supreme and recurring irony of political organisation, that it is precisely from the moment that the interests of the community as a whole are taken into account that individual rights are put most seriously at risk.

The works of Bodin and Belloy would have a wider impact in the following century not least in England where the former's ideas would help to shape the great intellectual design of Thomas Hobbes and the latter's would support Charles I on his stiff-necked journey to the scaffold. There would be other influences too, stemming from another crisis in western Europe contemporaneous with the religious wars in France, the revolt of the Netherlands.

The similarities between the two crises are striking. The same basic causes were at the root of both conflicts and the outcome in the two countries was less dissimilar than might at first appear. The privileged groups opposing the policies of the king of Spain were not exactly comparable with those in France, for in the Low Countries the urban merchant families vied with the nobility for social distinction and surpassed them in economic power. But if the emphasis was different, the underlying causes of friction were not. The high nobility, lords of the Golden Fleece, resented Philip II's refusal to allow his council of state in the Netherlands, of which they were members, to become an effective governing body. Instead he insisted on ruling through his own alien nominees and in pushing through policies, like the reorganisation of ecclesiastical boundaries in 1561, which added to noble resentment by putting episcopal nominations beyond their reach. Such measures threatened the privileges of towns as well as of noblemen, and it was soon clear that long-held rights were being ignored in Madrid in the interests of Philip's imperial role. And so the Dutch revolt began with the resistance of those privileged classes and communities which resented the growth of royal interference and felt secure enough in their rights to challenge it. Nor were they departing in this from the traditional Habsburg view of empire, recently expressed in this way in reference to Charles V: 'He was no Alexander or Napoleon who had conquered his empire but the hereditary and legitimate ruler of each of his states, whose laws and customs he

had sworn to maintain.'[14] His successor in Spain, Philip, did not
share his father's universalist spirit, partly because he inherited
only half an empire, though it is an historical irony that the
anachronistic regime of the Viennese Habsburgs should survive
for two hundred years longer than that of their initially more
étatiste-minded cousins in Madrid. Cardinal Granvelle, Philip's
representative as president of the council of state, shrewdly
perceived as early as 1559 the beginning of an alliance between
nobles and merchants in defence of their privileges — most
characteristically expressed in the 'Joyous Entry' of Brabant —
which boded ill for the future stability of this part of Philip's
empire.[15]

However, the situation in the Netherlands was complicated
even further by other factors, making the Dutch a very special
case and their successful revolt against the Habsburgs one of the
decisive elements in the evolution of the modern state. Its
geographical position gave it a measure of protection, especially
in view of Philip's inability to make quick decisions, when
indeed he was able to make them at all.[16] Of more importance
was the economic prosperity with its international commercial
repercussions which grew out of the geography of the Low
Countries. It bred a sense of independence, then resentment and
finally a spirit of local patriotism which spread through the
whole community and revealed itself in violent anti-Spanish
sentiment. On the other hand, many of the lesser nobility faced
economic ruin as rising prices destroyed the balance between
their extravagant way of life and their diminishing resources,
and they were willing, therefore, to throw in their lot with the
wealthy merchant oligarchies of the towns in the knowledge
that they had little to lose by doing so and possibly much to gain.
For their part, the town regents found such an alliance increasingly
attractive. They had much more to lose and as Philip sought to
bring the rebellious provinces to heel they seemed increasingly
likely to lose it. The Netherlanders' *bête noir,* the duke of Alva,
wrote to the king in 1568, 'The towns must be punished for their
rebelliousness with the loss of their privileges; a goodly sum
must be squeezed out of private persons; a permanent tax obtained

from the States of the country.'[17] Shortly afterwards he announced his intention of establishing the abortive Tenth Penny tax of ten per cent of the value of every article sold.

As we have already observed, the third and crucial element in the revolt of the Netherlands was the introduction of Calvinism. Again the parallel with the French experience is close: the reformed religion offered an efficient, indeed a ruthless organisation with which to confront the equally ruthless government of Alva. It offered an alternative and seemingly more attractive ideology to wealthy Dutch traders with their eyes on commerce and impoverished Dutch gentlemen with their eyes on the old church's wealth, than the unbending Catholicism of Philip II, increasingly identified in the Low Countries as the philosophy of an oppressive regime. It recruited popular support for the incipient revolt of the Dutch grandees from a wide range of urban artisans, fishermen and sailors who had had to support the heavy taxation necessary to sustain the war with France.

However, although religious dissent played a large part in the revolt there was, of course, much more at stake than Philip II's professed concern for 'the preservation of the Catholic faith and the honour of the apostolic see'.[18] As the revolt gathered momentum and revulsion against Philip's policies turned towards the rejection of Philip himself as ruler, the Dutch found themselves moving into uncharted terrain and their progress became cautious and tentative. William of Orange himself, and his noble lieutenants, were slow to renounce their loyalty to the king, not merely because their upbringing and background made them natural supporters of legitimate authority, but because few Netherlanders could envisage a substitute for ultimate royal sovereignty. It is possible that events would have turned out very differently if, instead of sending the duke of Alva, Philip had carried out his original intention of returning to the Netherlands in person in 1567. Alva's unwilling successor as governor, Don Luis de Requesens, wondered in 1573 whether by holding out the promise of the Infante as the eventual ruler of the Low Countries Philip might persuade the Netherlanders to end their revolt.[19] He understood that its leaders wanted not independence but a guarantee that their rights would not be distorted by the centripetal attraction of Madrid. Three years later, in the Pacification of Ghent, Philip's authority was still explicitly, if ambiguously, recognised though he himself refused to countenance the provisions of this agreement between all the provinces of the Low Countries. Even after the subsequent separation of North and South brought about by the military successes of Alexander Farnese and the split within the rebel ranks between popular Calvinist extremists and Erasmian aristocrats and patricians, the illusion of princely sovereignty persisted as the States-General offered the leadership of the country first to the duke of Anjou in 1581 and then to the earl of Leicester in 1586. These decisions, which bore little relevance to the real situation and appear extraordinary to later observers, indicate how confused contemporaries were about the nature of the revolt and its true implications in terms of political organisation. Nor is it in the least surprising that that should be so. The pressure of events induced pragmatic solutions, not a coherent philosophy. Yet, as in France during the same period, ideas were present, obscurely perceived and ambiguously expressed, that would in the end explain and justify the political reality.

The first indication may be found in the proposals made on behalf of William of Orange to an unauthorized meeting of the States of Holland held at Dordrecht in 1572. The view accepted up to this time by William and his followers is restated in article eight:

His Grace has no other purpose than to see that, under the lawful and worthy government of the King of Spain, as Duke of Brabant, Lorraine and Limburg, Count of Flanders, Holland, Zealand, etc., the power, authority and prestige of the Estates may be restored to their former state, in accordance with the privileges and rights which the king has sworn to maintain in these countries.

But the following three articles point in a different direction. By article nine the states were enjoined not to enter into any agreement with the king or his representatives 'without securing His Grace's advice, consent, and agreement upon it', and article ten offered a reciprocal guarantee from William that he would not act without the states' approval. Finally in article eleven he recommended that the deputies should each swear eternal loyalty to him and in return his representative would swear, on his behalf, to remain true to this newly established compact between the prince and the states.[20] Where, in all this, was true sovereignty to be found? With the states, whose representatives were being asked to pass judgment on these proposals but who spoke only for Holland, not for all the provinces in revolt against Spain, and who were in any case being asked for a more comprehensive oath of loyalty than William would vouchsafe in return? With William who, though taking the initiative, was evidently prepared to allow his own freedom of action to be limited by the prior need to obtain the states' approval? Or finally, with the king of Spain, still, by a legal fiction, the nominal sovereign, though that fiction was wearing very thin by 1572? The assembly of Dordrecht made it appear even more ridiculous by recognising William as stadtholder of Holland, that is, as the king's lieutenant in the province, though the king himself had already removed him from the post.

Matters were scarcely clarified in the Union of Utrecht (1579), which, more than any other legal document, came to signify the formal establishment of the United Provinces. Its basic element was the indissoluble union of the northern provinces which would henceforth provide a federal body within which each province would continue to enjoy its traditional liberties, apparently an arrangement of interlocking sovereign states, with ultimate sovereignty in the basic matters of war, peace and taxation affecting the whole union, depending upon the unanimous support of its constituent parts. But that was not quite the situation for, in the not unlikely event of disagreement on these vital matters, power to make the final decision was to lie with the various stadtholders. If they failed to agree amongst themselves an extraordinary procedure was proposed: 'they shall name impartial assessors or deputies of their own choice, and the parties shall be held to accept the decisions made by the stadtholders in this manner'.[21] It is true that the document did not set out to establish a new state and such provisions were envisaged only as temporary measures in the fight against Spain, not as the bases of the future constitutional practice of the United Provinces. Nevertheless, the complete failure of those delegates who drafted the document to grasp the essence of the struggle in which they were involved — the location of sovereignty in the Netherlands — is remarkable. As for the authority of the king of Spain, that was made no clearer by the decision, incorporated in the Union, to use the revenue emanating from the royal domain in the provinces concerned, as a contribution towards their defence, presumably against the king's own troops.

Finally, in 1581, the States-General rejected the sovereignty of the king of Spain, in an important document though one still vitiated by an overall confusion of ideas. As in the *Vindiciae* the idea that the rights of the community were of primary importance and the authority of the prince ought to be employed in guaranteeing those rights, a complete *bouleversement* of earlier thinking, was explicitly maintained: ' . . . subjects are not created by God for the sake of the prince . . . but rather that the prince is established for his subjects' sake (for without them he would not be a prince) . . .'. If the prince did not respect the property of the subject (and property included, of course, the subject's rights, privileges and liberties) then he no longer merited their obedience. For that reason, therefore, the States-General solemnly declared their intention no longer to recognise Philip II, 'in any matters concerning the principality, supremacy, jurisdiction, or domain of these Low Countries, nor to use or permit others to use his name as Sovereign Lord over them after this time'.[22] But the implications of Bodin's work had not yet permeated the Netherlands and the fact therefore that the states had not only the will to reject but also the ability to implement their rejection of an alien regime, was not interpreted as an indication that the crisis of authority had already been resolved without recourse to an outside agency. On the contrary, such an agency still seemed necessary to guarantee those rights for which the Netherlanders had been fighting, and so, by the same document, the United Provinces placed themselves under the leadership and government of the duke of Anjou. Though the governed were demanding parity with the governor, and though force was demonstrably the decisive factor in producing this change, traditional personal and patrimonial forms still seemed the most acceptable stereotype by which to make it public; what it also disguised, ironically, was the fact that the interest of the community as a whole in preserving the political order by whatever means might be necessary — the argument of reason of state — was accelerating the movement away from the personal to the impersonal, from the standards of private morality to those of public amorality, from the hands of illusory chieftains to the real source of power whose whereabouts was still not clear to contemporaries. The Dutch awaited Grotius to match the clarity of Bodin's vision.

Eventually the states of Holland, by far the most important economically of the rebellious provinces, took the lead, publishing a declaration in 1587 in which they asserted their own sovereignty and out of this provincial stand grew the ultimate union of the seven states of the independent United Provinces, each of them free and sovereign in its own right. The new machinery of government scarcely matched up to the novelty of the situation and were its effectiveness not a matter of historical fact it would seem an ill-fated attempt to satisfy conflicting interests, haphazard, cumbersome and parochial, as an English historian of the Dutch has recently and accurately observed.[23] Because of the sovereign authority vested separately in all seven provinces there was frequent need to refer back in the decision-making process from the States-General to the provinces and to the towns. And there were great differences in outlook and policy between urban-dominated provinces like Holland and those like Gelderland in which the nobility were preponderant and Friesland with its strong representation of small landowners. Yet the arrangement did work because the original intention of the Dutch, to preserve intact those rights and privileges universally symbolised by the Joyous Entry of Brabant, could only be achieved in this way, by those who dominated affairs in the various provinces, and who by definition therefore were the chief possessors of property and privilege, taking the defence and maintenance of these things into their own hands. In that sense the Dutch revolt was a conservative affair for, by severing their connections with the king of Spain, the northern provinces were opting for what was traditional and familiar rather than revolutionary. Though it would be perverse to ignore the fact that the implications of their revolt would be far-reaching in the effect that it had on European political ideas and practices, the intention of those who succeeded — and, as in France, there was a more genuinely democratic movement that failed — was not revolutionary, and the marks of their political, economic and social conservatism may be traced through the seventeenth century and beyond. In the view of one distinguished historian of the Netherlands, Hobbes's *Leviathan* was an anachronism in the Dutch Republic of his own day.[24]

The new political order worked too because, in practice, effective sovereignty lay with the merchant oligarchy of the most prosperous province, Holland, and of its most prosperous city, Amsterdam. Although Bodin established that sovereignty by its nature was indivisible, the Dutch succeeded in adding significantly to the complexity of the concept. They managed to refine the idea, to establish a kind of inner sovereignty which not even Bodin himself had fully comprehended. This nuclear concept depended upon an element which he did understand very well, that of force, not the force of arms but of wealth and commerce. In the short period between 1585 and 1622 the population of Amsterdam rose from a mere 30 000 to more than 100 000 as her economic prosperity grew. The Dutch carrying trade between the Baltic and the Bay of Biscay, exchanging grain, timber, iron and copper for salt and herring, was extended into the Mediterranean and then pushed further afield into the colonial preserves of Spain and Portugal. Holland contributed some fifty-eight per cent of the Provinces' combined budget; almost half the members of the governing body of the Dutch East India Company, founded in 1602, were nominated by the Amsterdam chamber of commerce; and from 1609 the bank of Amsterdam pumped the wealth of four continents through the body politic. But even more important were the economic implications of the new republic's political organisation. The Dutch regent class, for whom a king in Madrid had proved

too inhibiting an experience, were unwilling to contemplate one
nearer home and so the Netherlands emerged as a merchant
republic, geared to the commercial interests of its sponsors. The
directors of the East India Company were all members of town
councils, provincial estates and the States-General and some of
them were also directors of the bank of Amsterdam.[25] The
Dutch East India Company had the right to make treaties and
alliances in the name of the States-General, to appoint military
and judicial officials, and its employees took two oaths, one to
the States-General and one to the Company. Yet this politico-
economic *rapport* was only achieved at the expense of military
vulnerability at the very time when external pressures on this
rash interloper were likely to be even stronger than among
existing powers. It is true that, in moments of military crisis
when the Republic's survival seemed threatened, the hegemony
of the dominant merchant class was disputed by the house of
Orange, but it was never overthrown. For, in the final analysis,
the princes preferred to accept the privileged, though ancillary,
status which history had bequeathed to them in the Low Countries
rather than risk losing it altogether by challenging this same
class upon whom the stability of the political order depended.[26]
The epicentre of Dutch sovereignty, therefore, lay with the
regent class of the province of Holland.

Consequently the Dutch revolt is instructive in underlining
what Bodin had already observed and the French Wars of
Religion clearly indicated, that the possession of sovereign power
is the necessary prerequisite of political stability. But it also tells
us more than that in demonstrating that the precise location of
sovereignty is not always readily defined. Bodin accepted that
sovereignty was in close alliance with force, at the root of all
political organisation, though man's natural unwillingness
voluntarily to submit to tyranny always tended to disguise that
fact. The Dutch revolt suggested that force might also push
sovereignty into a hitherto unsuspected inner core, like a Russian
matryoshka doll, one replica within another. The more elusive
the ultimate source of power, the further removed from the
personal, patrimonial authority of the prince, the more vague

and impersonal would its justification become. The growing authority of the princes had forced them to justify their additional powers in terms of *raison d'état* and in parts of Europe they carried that argument successfully through critical times. In the Low Countries, however, the crisis was resolved differently. These provinces were virtually a colonial possession containing powerful elements whose interests were so at variance with those of their sovereign that they were unwilling to accept his view of reason of state. Ultimately they succeeded in replacing him altogether but they could only justify their revolt by substituting their own concept of interest of state, which meant no more than the preservation of the new *status quo,* in terms borrowed from earlier, princely usage but now totally lacking in precision and practically devoid of meaning.

THE QUEST FOR SOVEREIGNTY (II):
COMMERCIAL RIVALRY AND THE ENGLISH
EXPERIENCE

A new and potentially crucial factor in the emergence of the modern state — international commercial rivalry — arose out of the developments in the Low Countries. It was the Dutch Revolt which forced European governments to concern themselves with the novel political and international implications of trading activity. Until late in the sixteenth century the chief concern of princes in the field of trade and commerce was to extract financial resources adequate to ensure internal security. On occasion the measures taken towards that end affected other countries, though usually as an indirect, almost irrelevant result of narrowly domestic considerations. Philip II's attempt to impose the Tenth Penny tax in the Netherlands and Elizabeth I's revocation of Hanse privileges to assist the merchant adventurers were decisions of this sort, although one was of far greater long-term significance than the other; while in France at a slightly later date Henry IV's adviser, Laffemas, was of the opinion that French interests would be best served by the virtual cessation of foreign trade. In Sweden Gustav Vasa adhered to a medieval view of the economy, where payment in kind was more common than in money, a view which he could only sustain by adopting an extremely parochial stance towards his country's commercial activities. In Muscovy, although Ivan the Terrible was profiting from a growing export market in Russian furs, he was content to leave the organisation of the industry to a remarkable entrepreneurial family, the Stroganov, whose own private trade with Europe was so extensive that one of its members, Anika, contrived to become the tsar's personal supplier of Italian wines.[1] At rare moments governments did take a direct hand: there is a fourteenth century example of Edward III putting an embargo on English wool to intimidate the Flemings and one of Louis XI in the following century seeking to exclude English merchants from Bordeaux.[2] But even Castile's acquisition of her American colonies and the consequent mercantilist measures undertaken by Ferdinand and Isabella — the prohibition to export gold and silver, the strict control of incoming bullion, the navigation laws — failed to stimulate a fundamentally new attitude. Indeed, although Philip II of Spain and Elizabeth of England later found themselves involved in what was virtually economic warfare, both sides preferred to see 'the violence and insolence of subjects' at the root of the problem, rather than the conflicting policies of the two governments. Philip wrote to his ambassador in London in August 1566:

You will use every effort with the Queen and Council to stop the robberies which English pirates are constantly committing on our subjects, which should not be permitted, since between me and the Queen such perfect peace and concord exist, and it is not right that the violence and insolence of subjects should cast any shadow thereupon. We should rather try mutually to punish such subjects so severely that it should be an example for the rest to preserve the amity which exists between us.[3]

The situation changed dramatically as the Dutch substituted, for the military might which they lacked, an aggressive and expansionist trading spirit. They sought security in a new way and in so doing found a new enemy, England. Within weeks of the *de facto* achievement of Dutch independence in 1609 the threat to English interests was sufficiently apparent for James I to issue a proclamation to the effect that 'no person of what nation or quality soever, being not our natural born subject, be permitted to fish upon any of our coasts and seas . . . until they have . . . demanded and obtained licences from us'.[4] Shortly afterwards, in 1613 and 1615, two colonial conferences were held, ostensibly between the two countries' East India Companies but the Dutch made it clear that this merchants' quarrel was an affair of state. The English side was forced to follow the Dutch line and the discussions between businessmen came to be supervised by the politicians: the Dutch commissioners carried letters of credence from the States-General and their English counterparts were appointed by a commission of the privy council.[5] In fact the feeling was growing in England that the government had no option but to intervene in the regulation of economic affairs, and in particular to concern itself with the problem of the sovereignty of the sea. Sir Walter Raleigh had already succintly observed that 'whosoever commands the sea commands the trade; whoever commands the trade of the world commands the riches of the world, and consequently the world itself', and it was clear enough in early Stuart England that the Dutch fishing industry was laying siege to the British coast.[6] Behind it was a steadily increasing mercantile fleet threatening to take over the English import trade which would inevitably encourage and require the growth of Dutch naval power. In 1609 James I had recognised the importance of the British shipping industry for both trade and security, hailing it as 'a maine pillar of this Kingdome', and in 1620 he acknowledged the need to 'maintain and increase . . . the strength of our navy . . . as principal sinews for the strength and service of our crown and kingdom', thus following the advice given to his predecessor some thirty years earlier: 'convert your treasure for . . . the arming of ships and men of war, that may defend you, sith princes' treasures serve only to that end and lie they never so fast nor so full in their chests, can no waies so defend them'.[7] No doubt James had mixed feelings about this new political rivalry for he had once allowed himself an extravagant panegyric on these same Dutchmen:

Were they not an ill-fedde and scragged people, in comparison of the inestimable wealth and prosperity . . . to which they are now raysed and mounted by the mercifull blessing of God, since the darkness of Poperie hath beene scattered and the bright Sunne of the gospel hath shined in those Countryes?[8]

Alas for James's enthusiasm, there was no room in the new

politics for the 'bright sunne of the gospel' when its wonders were performed so efficaciously and perversely in the service of a potential enemy.

In step with the political practice, itself the product of new ideas, went the theoretical arguments and justifications. Grotius published *Mare Liberum* in 1609 and Selden replied in 1618 with *Mare Clausum*, though it was not published until 1636, the former arguing for complete freedom of the seas for all nations to exploit, the latter making the case for the crown's sovereignty over the British seas. *Mare Clausum* was interpreted by the Dutch as an official statement of the British point of view and was formally refuted by the States-General. Theory and practice, economics and politics were closely intermingled: Sir Edward Coke observed that

whosoever will encroach upon him [the king] by sea, will do it by land also when they see their time. To such presumption *Mare Liberum* gave the first warning-piece, which must be answered with a defense of *Mare Clausum*: not so much by discourses, as by the louder language of a powerful navy, to be better understood when overstrained patience seeth no hope of preserving her right by other means.[9]

Nor had the merchant, Thomas Mun, who wrote his famous treatise while serving as a trade commissioner for James I any doubts about the importance of maintaining the country's international commercial standing:

. . . many well-governed states highly countenance the profession, and carefully cherish the action [of foreign trade] not only with Policy to encrease it, but also with power to protect it from all foreign injuries: because they know it is a Principle in reason of state to maintain and defend that which doth support them.

He also implied a distinction, though as yet far from clear-cut, between the state and the sovereign:

. . . for we may exchange either amongst ourselves, or with strangers; if amongst ourselves, the Commonwealth cannot be enriched thereby; for the gain of one subject is the loss of another. And if we exchange with strangers, then our profit is the gain of the Commonwealth. Yet by none of these ways can the king receive any benefit in his customs.[10]

From the English point of view the situation deteriorated as the mid-century approached. Maritime trade was at a desperately low level as the Dutch succeeded in breaking into the North American, West Indian and Irish trade, and English ships were virtually excluded from the Mediterranean and the Baltic. Cromwell's answer was to strengthen the navy, which was not a new idea, and to pass the 1651 Navigation Act, which was.[11] It enunciated the doctrine that goods coming into England should be brought direct from their country of origin either in the ships of that country or in English ones, and was the starting point for a whole series of similar enactments which together signified that the English had learnt their Dutch lesson well. Henceforth English mercantile policy would depend upon parliamentary statute, not the haphazard granting of privileges to private companies. A short time before, in 1630, Charles I had proclaimed his intention of maintaining the Eastland Company in its privileges and immunities, 'well knowing how much the supporting and encouragement of this company in particular imports the service and benefit of his Majesty and the state'.[12] However, Thomas Mun had already questioned the advantages of such a policy and in 1651 the government took steps, not to remedy the king's lack of 'any benefit in his customs', since it had already removed the king, but to assert full political control through the customs officers over the revenues to be raised from a flourishing import trade. In the following years the political regulation of trade went further: in 1672 a Council of Trade and Plantations was established, composed of statesmen rather than merchants, 'more like a department of state than any previous council', with orders to consider 'of the several advantages that may accrue unto these our kingdoms by giving way . . . to a more open and free trade than that of companies and corporations';[13] in 1696 a permanent board of trade was set up and a statistical department under the Inspector-General of Imports and Exports allowed the government to exercise a close supervision over the trading community.

Thus England succeeded in the course of the seventeenth century in overcoming the competition of her great trading rival, the United Provinces, by striking at her carrying trade through the Navigation Acts and also by waging three trade wars in the second half of the century from which she emerged as the dominant European sea power. Underlying this success was a fundamental change in outlook. Whereas in the Low Countries considerations of commerce continued to dominate politics precisely the opposite came to be true of England. The Navigation Act of 1651 was not the result of pressure mounted by the merchant corporations; on the contrary, it was rather an indication that such companies had had their day. The nature of the Dutch social and political structure on the other hand made a similar adjustment difficult for them. De Witt wrote in 1662 that the most advantageous thing for the state would be a simple treaty of commerce and navigation without any obligation of mutual defense, and in 1702 his countryman, Pieter de la Court remarked that:

All the rulers in Holland are derived of parents that have lived by the fisheries, manufactories, traffic or navigation and so their children after them; and that the said rulers do still daily to maintain their families find it proper to marry their children to rich merchants or their children. So that such rulers, whether considered in themselves by their consanguinity or affinity, are in all respects interested in the welfare or illfare of the fisheries, manufactories, manufactures, traffic and navigation of this country. And accordingly we must believe that the said rulers and magistrates under a free government, whether in their own cities or at the assemblies of Holland, will by their counsels and resolutions, endeavour to preserve and increase the same means of subsistence for the country in general.[14]

Though both countries moved closer to statehood during their protracted struggle, this crucial difference in approach made England the more convincing prototype. Her government had taken over the detailed regulation of an area of activity which it had previously considered of only peripheral importance and was submitting it to ever closer bureaucratic control. In effecting this transformation the idea of the overriding national interest was bound to gain currency and assist in separating the government's, or the crown's authority, from that of the state. Yet once more we must beware of bolting our fences for in 1660 Charles II regained his customs dues for life and it took another political revolution to restore fully the momentum of earlier years. In the Netherlands there was still some way to go despite the unique origins and the subsequent precocity of the Dutch rise to power, neither of which should be forgotten. Despite Sir William Temple's remark in his *Observations upon the United Provinces* in 1678 that 'this Nation in particular . . . had not ever been without some head, under some title or other; but always an head subordinate to their laws and customs *and to the sovereign power of the state*',[15] the Dutch commercial bureaucracy lagged nevertheless behind the English. They were still farming out their excise dues in the eighteenth century, and their trading interests regularly threatened to undermine the Provinces' security: in the war of independence with Spain Amsterdam merchants invested in Dunkirk privateers who preyed on Dutch shipping; in the first Franco-Dutch war of 1672–78 the Dutch provided Louis XIV's armies with all their powder and lead; and during the Anglo-Dutch wars the Amsterdammers supplied the English navy with cordage and sailcloth.[16]

Although the Dutch and the English were the chief protagonists in this long drawn out commercial struggle, the mightiest European power in the seventeenth century, France, was also drawn towards the economic battle-front. In his *Traicté de l'Oeconomie Politique,* of 1615, Montchrétien pointed out that whatever right an individual might have to take part in trade, the prince had an overriding authority to manipulate it as he saw fit for reasons of state, and this plea for political control of the country's commerce was shortly afterwards reflected in Richelieu's decision to establish a royal navy for the protection of French coasts and maritime trade, a reversal of his decision in 1624 to entrust the task to a private fleet.[17] Yet France remained primarily a military power, preoccupied with her land frontiers and far less concerned than the English with the growing Dutch stranglehold on her ports, and while she remained an ally of the Netherlands against Spain, there was little likelihood of the French government responding favourably to an appeal like that drawn up in 1645 by the merchants of Nantes. They complained bitterly to the King's Council that the Dutch in that port

assert that they have the same privileges as the native residents of the city and that if anyone puts a hand on them, they will complain to their own States and will call the public powers to their assistance. They lodge their appeals directly with the Council and call upon their agents and ambassadors to intercede for them on every occasion. Their envoys are themselves all merchants and make the least quarrel into matters of state . . . they are now so presumptuous that they claim that they are dispensed from the laws and ordinances of the French state and may infringe the statutes and privileges of the cities in which they reside. . . .[18]

After 1648, when the Dutch made their peace with Spain, the attitude of the French government did change and the United Provinces found themselves subjected to economic assault as well as to direct military pressure. National political considerations came to dominate French commercial activities as first Fouquet and then Colbert imposed a series of protectionist measures aimed primarily at the Dutch but most effective in fact against the English. As a result of that growing imbroglio a number of prominent English merchants published their 'Scheme of Trade' in 1674 to demonstrate that British imports from France exceeded her exports to France by almost £1 million per annum. A tariff war between the two countries ensued which in turn fed and helped to mould Anglo-French animosity in the late seventeenth and early eighteenth centuries.[19]

In the Baltic region at about the same time a similar, smaller-scale struggle was taking place with the Swedes engaged in a determined effort to control trade into and out of Muscovy, not only by shutting her off altogether from the Baltic shore, but also by seeking to wrest Novgorod and Pskov, the two key trading centres of north-western Russia, from the newly established Romanov dynasty. Having failed in that ambition they began the construction of a port, Nyen, at the mouth of the Neva and their merchants infiltrated into Pskov and Novgorod. Later in the century, during the Anglo-Dutch wars they went to the extraordinary lengths of seeking to persuade one or other of the combatants to destroy the port of Archangel, Muscovy's only sea-outlet to the west, whose volume of trade was derisory in comparison with that of the Baltic ports.[20]

None of this is to suggest, of course, that in France and Sweden, any more than in England and the Netherlands, the idea of the state as an abstract entity had fully crystallized in the seventeenth century. It was precisely the highly personalised nature of his rule which so antagonised Louis XIV's critics, and the king himself consistently overlooked the financial implications of his policies; while in Sweden an impoverished nobility, anxious to obtain new sources of wealth and political power, may well have prompted the policy of Baltic encirclement.[21] Nevertheless, the tendency to make mercantile policy *vis-à-vis* foreign powers a government matter, added weight in that direction and helped, in the crucial area of inter-state relationships, to stamp the first faint yet indelible impress. The birth of modern international law is closely associated with disputes over trade and the sovereignty of the sea, and it is significant that of the various treatises written on the subject around the end of the sixteenth century and the beginning of the seventeenth, it is the work of a Dutchman, Grotius, that sounds most familiar to our ears: 'For whatever the king does in acts belonging to his kingly office should be considered in the same way as if the state did them.'[22]

The mention of Grotius brings us back to the domestic crises affecting France and the Netherlands. In both countries a profound thinker finally made coherent ideas and concepts which were only dimly perceived, if perceived at all, by most of the participants in the revolutionary movements of the later sixteenth century. Interestingly enough, Grotius continued to link sovereignty with kingship, an indication perhaps of the new republic's unwillingness to see itself in revolutionary guise. His initial definition is straightforward: 'That power is called sovereign whose actions are not subject to the legal control of another'. However, he then goes further, elaborating the concept along the lines of the graduated sovereignty discussed above:

The subject of a power is either common or special. Just as the body is a common, the eye a special subject of the power of sight, so the state, which we have defined above as a perfect association, is the common subject of sovereignty. . . . The special subject is one or more persons, according to the laws and customs of each nation.[23]

Here he implicitly accepts the idea of the community of interest between ruler and ruled, with the balance now adjusted in favour of the latter; and indeed, in a later passage he is quite explicit on the subject: 'For the sovereign power, which resides in the king as the head, remains in the people as the whole body, of which the head is a part.' Nor, finally, does he shrink from recognising the major implications of sovereignty in respect to the common interest, first in the ultimate appeal to reason of state: 'But the right of subjects is subordinate to that of eminent domain so far as the public interest may require', and 'We must note that recourse is had to the right of eminent domain, not indiscriminately, but only in so far as this is to the common advantage in a civil government, which, even when regal, is not despotic.' Grotius enlarges upon this theme:

I have said elsewhere that the property of subjects belongs to the state under the right of eminent domain; in consequence the state, or he who represents the state, can use the property of subjects, and even destroy it or alienate it, not only in case of direct need, which grants even to private citizens a measure of right over others' property, but also for the sake of the public advantage; and to the public advantage those very persons who formed the body politic should be considered as desiring that private advantage should yield.

Secondly, he acknowledges that such considerations can have no basis in, nor relevance to the accepted standards of morality:

The moral goodness or badness of an action, especially in matters relating to the State, is not suited to a division into parts; such qualities frequently are obscure, and difficult to analyse. In consequence, the utmost confusion would prevail in case the king on the one side, and the people on the other, under the pretext that an act is good or bad, should be trying to take cognizance of the same matter, each by virtue of its power.[24]

The resolution of the Dutch crisis seems strikingly different from the French solution, and so it was in some obvious respects. Yet the resemblances between the two are equally remarkable. In France, as in the Netherlands, what was at issue was the ultimate location and justification of power, and under the pressure of events in this crucial area each country edged towards the other. In outward forms, of course, they remained poles apart, though even here the long sustained influence of the conservative traditions of the Low Countries and of their Spanish adversaries were not readily eradicated. But there was yet another crisis brewing, this time in England, which differed in important respects though not fundamentally from both these other two.

The reasons for the opposition to the English crown were closely comparable with the three-fold motives of the Dutch and French dissidents. The powerful message of radical Protestantism — Puritanism in England — provided a dynamic justification for opposition and though the crown's official Anglicanism did not represent a threat to the reformed church on the scale of that posed by Philip of Spain or the Catholic rulers of France, neither did it convince ardent disciples of Geneva of its commitment to thoroughgoing Protestantism. Similarly the crown's financial difficulties — even in peacetime — were growing as rising prices, inherited war debts and the need to sustain an increasingly centralised and complex government bureaucracy over-taxed the royal resources. In wartime the situation became very difficult indeed and the first two Stuart kings found themselves embroiled in struggles with the House of Commons as they sought to make capital of a variety of financial expedients: additional revenue from customs dues, forced loans, sale of office, ship money. It is Parliament, and the House of Commons in particular, which brings us to the third element, that of status, and links it with the other two. In early Stuart England the House of Commons was dominated by the men of property, landowning gentry and merchants who were directly affected by such royal enterprises but whose resentment was also fostered by the predominantly puritan sympathies of the House and by its members' awareness of the status which parliament had come to enjoy since the Henrician Reformation. These factors together encouraged not merely negative opposition to the crown's financial and religious policies but the affirmation of a positive constitutional position which directly challenged the authoritarianism of the Tudors and the divine-right principles of James I. To the latter's cautious

observation that 'in-case necessitie of warres, or other extra-
ordinaries compell you to lift Subsidies, doe it as rarely as ye can',
the Commons countered in the Petition of Right with the
demand, 'that no man hereafter be compelled to make or yield
any gift, loan, benevolence, tax or such like charge without
common consent by Act of Parliament'.[25]

In this crisis which led to the Civil War and eventually to the
execution of the king himself, the underlying issue was also the
same as in France and the Low Countries: it was a question of
where sovereignty lay, of whether the prince could continue to
justify his much inflated authority despite the antagonisms
aroused by such an accretion of power. However, there were
several aspects of the situation in England which were not to be
found on the continent of Europe and which help to explain the
different, and more radical, form of the English solution. One
was the growth of the concept — so brilliantly analysed by
E. H. Kantorowicz — of the king's two bodies, a concept which
in certain circumstances might be employed to challenge the
unique personal supremacy of the king. According to Edmund
Plowden's Elizabethan interpretation of the idea, 'the King has
in him two Bodies, *viz.*, a Body natural, and a Body politic . . .
his Body politic is a Body that cannot be seen or handled, con-
sisting of Policy and Government, and constituted for the
Direction of the People, and the Management of the public weal'.
In addition, the body politic was considered immortal, passing
from monarch to monarch upon the death of the natural body.
Bearing in mind the acrimonious relationship which subsequently developed between king and parliament, it is not difficult
to detect the extension of this same doctrine in the declaration
of the Lords and Commons of May, 1642: 'It is acknowledged
that the King is the Fountain of Justice and Protection, but
the Acts of Justice and Protection are not exercised in his own
Person, nor depend upon his pleasure, but by his Courts and his
Ministers who must do their duty therein, though the King in his
own Person should forbid them': hence the Puritan slogan of
'fighting the king to defend the King'.[26]

The second and major idiosyncrasy on the English political

scene was the existence of statute as the supreme law of the land, enabling the king, Lords and Commons, collectively to ordain whatever they chose to ordain, however novel, however difficult to reconcile with existing beliefs and practices. With this weapon Henry VIII had severed England's links with Rome and so long as the king remained in full control of the political situation he could employ its formidable support to consolidate his authority further. However when the king found himself seriously at odds with the House of Commons he discovered that it had acquired a taste for statutory power, that its palate had been whetted rather than dulled by periods of abstinence and a restricted diet, and that its members were prepared to challenge the supremacy of the crown alone in the name of the king in parliament.

But what sort of animal was this 'king in parliament' which did ultimately emerge as the supreme power in the land? Did it truly represent the community whose interests the sovereign was expected to maintain? Its relationship with the governed was far more occluded than that posited by James I: 'I am the Husband, and all the whole Isle is my lawfull Wife.'[27] In fact, as we have already observed of the Low Countries, when the problem of sovereignty was at issue it was not always easy to penetrate to its innermost recesses. It did not always lie where it seemed, and though 'king in parliament' was a satisfactory constitutional formula masking the force applied by civil war, it was also a mask for that inner core of sovereignty which still awaited discovery in the working out of the new formula. In England therefore personal royal power, already under assault in the doctrine of the king's two bodies, was commuted into the impersonal doctrine of parliamentary sovereignty, a doctrine proclaiming the determination of a politically articulate group to share in the advantages bestowed by the new dogma of raison d'état, rather than to suffer from its application. As in the Low Countries this produced a new order which lacked precision and meaning in terms of what had gone before. Rather as the Copernican view of the universe destroyed the intimate relationship between man and the Almighty, leaving His whereabouts disturbingly vague and amorphous, so the toppling of the king from his central place in the political order left his subjects uncertain of their ultimate loyalty and identification. The time was fast approaching therefore when the enveloping concept of the impersonal state would become an acceptable holdall encompassing the aspirations of all the subjects. It was approaching more rapidly in England than in the United Provinces since the shift in authority could not be effected in England without radical and permanent change, for the king's role was closely bound up with the country's political fortunes whereas in the quasi-colonial situation of the Dutch it was possible, once the irritating rein of royal authority from Madrid had been cut, to proceed along familiar lines which came to overlie the revolutionary nature of the Dutch revolt. It may be too that the traditional basis of Dutch government exercised a restraining influence upon the new United Provinces while the arbitrary nature of statute and the lack of similar legally based traditions in England made her a readier candidate for further change.

What we have been describing in France, the United Provinces and England adds up to a general crisis but of a rather different kind from that so much debated by historians in recent years. This is a crisis arising out of the burgeoning power of the princes which brought to a head the question of where ultimate power lay and what that sovereignty meant in terms of political action. It is not a crisis narrowly concerned with the struggle for the economic or social advancement of one particular group, nor with the struggle for the conscience of Europe, though the elements of religion, economy and status all make their impact to differing degrees according to the vagaries of the particular situation. The main difficulty about the 'general crisis' thesis in fact is that in all its manifestations it seems not general enough but too particular. The general crisis indicated above on the other hand eschews particulars: to be taken seriously it requires the reader to accept that a variety of groups challenged the power of the prince with various motives and with varying results. All they had in common was a deep resentment against the princes' claim to maintain the *status quo* by effectively changing it in their own favour. Nor can this 'general crisis' be accurately dated to the mid-seventeenth century. In fact the centre of gravity should be located in the late sixteenth, though the crisis continues through the first half of the next century. Thus the critical period in Russia is the Time of Troubles following the death of Ivan the Terrible in 1584 and ending with the accession of Michael Romanov in 1613, a period in which the institution of tsardom, heavily backed by the Russian Orthodox church, succeeded in overcoming the threat to Muscovy's very identity posed by discontented and impoverished noblemen and gentry, and by peasant farmers in their flight from serfdom. Consequently in the seventeenth century sovereignty lay unequivocally with the tsar who had no legal sources of opposition to contend with and who was more truly the state therefore than ever Louis XIV could claim to be. The idea of the impersonal state, commanding the subjects' total loyalty, could be absorbed more readily into this political environment than it could in those countries where sovereignty had slipped away from the person of the prince into less clearly defined areas, but the distinction between the two cases is more apparent than real, for sovereignty remains in essence the ally of force which the tsar sought to justify no less than the burghers of Amsterdam or the gentry members of the Long Parliament in terms other than those of tyranny and despotism.

Of the other outbreaks which supporters of the 'general crisis' theme enunciate, the troubles in Catalonia and Portugal in the 1640s represent the failure of the Spanish crown, following the disasters of the Dutch revolt and the Thirty Years War, to combat the traditional hostility to central authority in the name of *raison d'état,* a failure which deprived the crown of the compromise solution achieved in France and robbed it of effective sovereignty. For the remainder of the Habsburgs' debilitating rule in Spain the idea of the state made no progress in the face of the old provincialism redolent of the days of Ferdinand of Aragon and the Emperor Charles V. In France the Frondes offer merely an epilogue to the more significant battles of the French Wars of

Religion: the king's position was not adversely affected by the events of 1648–52, nor were the arrangements tacitly agreed under Henry IV put seriously at risk. The English Revolution, though far more radical than the simultaneous disturbances across the Channel, should thus be seen not as the focal point of the whole 'general crisis' situation but as almost the concluding scene of a drama begun far earlier.

Finally, the long drawn out crisis of the kingdom of Poland began when the ruling Jagiellon dynasty came to an end with the death of Sigismund II in 1572. From that date the elective principle was re-established and in return for noble support candidates for the throne had to accept in advance certain restrictions upon their authority. In addition most of Poland's rulers after that date were foreigners, often preoccupied with the fortunes of their own lands to the detriment of their new acquisition. The first three monarchs after 1572 were Henry of Valois who spent only months in Poland before withdrawing to ascend the French throne as Henry III; Stephen Bathory whose foreign policy was greatly influenced by the desire to defend his native Transylvania against the Turks; and Sigismund Vasa who sought nothing so much as his family's Swedish crown. Consequently there was even less likelihood in Poland than in Spain of any shift towards the concept of an impersonal state; indeed the subsequent history of that country tends to carry it quite outside the scope of this enquiry.

6

TOWARDS THE LEVIATHAN

As the implications of these various episodes, this 'general crisis', became clearer in seventeenth-century Europe, some acute politicians and several giant intellectual figures added their contributions on varying levels of perception. In Spain the towering figure of the Count-Duke of Olivares is a disappointment in this respect, for although his attempts at coordinating the affairs of the Spanish Empire through Castile were more subtly conceived than those of his predecessors — owing something perhaps to the changing emphasis in favour of the community interest elaborated by Bodin — they still foundered on the rock of provincialism partly at least because he himself was not attuned to some of the other implications of Bodin's work. His preoccupation was with an older political concept, the fusion of interests between king and people which stopped short of the idea of authority exercised in the name of this union but outside the traditional limits: in short, he lacked the crucial concept of reason of state and his alternative was no longer compelling enough to save the Spanish Habsburgs from disaster.[1]

In France, however, Olivares' great contemporary, Cardinal Richelieu, saw matters very differently. He too inherited the changing view of the community interest as something deserving of more emphasis than the prince's interest alone. He writes in his *Testament Politique* of kings being established to maintain, not to ruin their subjects. He also faithfully reflects the compromise settlement emanating from the French Wars of Religion. Through the long first chapter he regularly refers to the king's state in highly personalised terms; nor has he any doubts about the location and nature of ultimate sovereignty: 'But it has to be borne in mind that there are many occasions when a minister, however powerful he may be, cannot produce certain effects because they require the voice of a sovereign and an absolute power.' Yet there is in this last admonition a clue to the other side of the coin to which Richelieu also frequently alludes, the king's need from time to time to step outside the rules of patri- monial obligation in pursuit of a more compelling if less clearly defined objective: 'In certain cases, where the welfare of the State is concerned, it is necessary to employ a vigorous authority which sometimes oversteps the usual rules of prudence and which it is sometimes impossible to keep clear of certain evils.'[2] The pursuit of this objective entitles the king to behave in a manner totally alien to that prescribed by the normal rules of justice of which he is the guarantor:

... although in the normal course of events justice requires authentic evidence, that is not the case in matters concerning the State for then what is apparent in a pressing situation must sometimes be regarded as sufficiently explained. ... On such occasions it is sometimes necessary to begin with the execution whereas in every other circumstance the right must be elucidated by witnesses or unimpeachable documents.

Richelieu is able, like Bodin, to capture in one brilliant aphorism the essence of sovereignty, thereby qualifying and interpreting everything else that he has to say about kingship in France: 'Qui a la force a souvent la raison en matière d'Etat.'[3]

Richelieu's views are faithfully reflected in the actions and writings of his royal successor and posthumous pupil, Louis XIV, who in 1661, in his memoirs for his son, noted that 'when war is necessary, it is in justice not merely permitted but commanded of kings'.[4] Louis retained throughout his long reign the mixed outlook which he had inherited and which may be summed up in the famous if apocryphal remark, 'L'Etat, c'est moi'. It is custo- mary to interpret this phrase in outright patrimonial terms with the emphasis upon the unrestrained power of the king to act as he personally saw fit; but it may be interpreted with equal validity in an almost completely opposite fashion, as indicating Louis' obligation to act in the interests of the state even when his own inclinations ran counter to such a course of action. In a study of his reign both interpretations find support. Towards the beginning of his personal rule the Treaty of the Pyrenees was primarily a dynastic settlement between the Bourbon and Habsburg families, arranging not only Louis' marriage to a Spanish Infanta but even the restoration of the rebel Condé's French estates. Towards the end of his reign Louis was still concerned with the dynastic implications of that treaty as he resorted to arms once more to assert his family's right to inherit the Spanish Empire. In between he pursued his policy of *la gloire,* which he saw not as mere military bombast but as the verdict of posterity on his struggle to bequeath to his heirs a state at least as strong and secure as when he inherited it: a fundamentally patrimonial concept. On the other hand there were indications of new and potentially conflicting ideas. The king himself inadvertently expressed this dichotomy when he wrote in 1661:

For indeed, my son, we must consider the good of our subjects far more than our own. They are almost a part of ourselves, since we are the head of a body and they are its members. It is only for their own advantage that we must give them laws, and our power over them must only be used by us in order to work more effectively for their happiness. It is wonderful to deserve from them the name of father along with that of master.

In the same year he observed, in writing of the handling of the state's finances: 'The prince alone should have sovereign direction over it because he alone has no fortune to establish, but that of the state, no acquisition to make except for the monarchy, no authority to strengthen other than that of the laws, no debts to pay besides the public ones, no friends to enrich save his people.'[5] By 1666 the king was precisely mirroring the view of Bodin and Grotius on the sovereign's ultimate right to dispose of his subjects' property: 'kings are absolute lords and naturally have free and full disposition of all the goods possessed by clergymen as well as by laymen, in order to use them at any time as wise administrators, that is, according to the general need of their state.'[6]

Before the end of his reign Louis was referring to 'the state' instead of 'my state', and presiding over a rapidly expanding bureaucracy.[7] Permanent depositories had been established to house state papers in the spheres of foreign affairs, war, the navy and the colonies, while in 1712 the king consented to the establishment of a political academy to train future diplomats in the service of the French state. In the negotiations with William III leading to the partition treaties of 1698 and 1700 Louis was apparently willing, in the interests of European peace and the balance of power, to settle the division of the Spanish Empire with one of the few monarchs who did not himself have a claim to that inheritance, a settlement suggesting that dynastic claims had to give way, at least on occasion, before considerations of more impersonal power politics. But only on occasion and in a confused fashion for Louis' starting point in the partition treaty negotiations and much of his subsequent argument, like his refusal to allow the elector of Bavaria to take over his dead son's share of the spoils, was based squarely on dynastic considerations, as was his later provocative and ill-judged recognition of the Old Pretender as James III.[8] The same partial perception is to be found in the political academy, which, though intended to create a professional corps of state diplomats, still dealt in the essentially dynastic coin of proprietory deeds, marriage settlements and inherited rights.[9]

Moreover, we have already observed the hazard of giving too much weight in isolation to bureaucratic developments. The archives in Simancas were established in 1545 yet, by the time of Louis XIV's reign, Spain had succumbed to the rudderless lethargy of a degenerate dynasty from which only the advent of the Bourbons would eventually arouse her. In the very last year of Spanish Habsburg rule there was still an unquestioning confidence behind Porto Carrero's assertion that 'Princes are the image of God and occupy His place on earth', a pithy and simplistic doctrine which in the Spanish context apparently left nothing more to be said.[10]

The failure of Louis XIV's successors to resolve the dichotomy inherent in their role, to disengage themselves altogether from the personal and patrimonial chain which anchored them, meant that in the long run quickening new currents would set them suddenly adrift and sweep them headlong into the abyss. It is beyond the scope of the present work to pursue those events to their conclusion but a final glimpse of the approaching conflict may be perceived in the regency of Philip of Orléans which followed Louis XIV's death. By then the element of reason of state, or high domain, 'le droit de transferer à Jean la propriété des biens de Pierre' in pursuit of the public good was well established, and Richelieu's *Testament Politique* provided the regent with a valuable *vade mecum* in the task of tutoring his young master, Louis XV.[11] But what interests were to be served by this reserve power of kingship? Were they to remain essentially dynastic as Cardinal Dubois' estimate of his own achievements seems to suggest: 'I have established a third Bourbon branch in the centre of Italy . . . on all sides I will have put tremendous impediments to the House of Austria'? Or, ironically, was the animosity felt by some dynastically minded Frenchmen towards the policies of Orléans and Dubois hastening the emergence of the idea of the impersonal state in whose interests the ruler would be required to act as the chief servant? That seems to be the direction in which one anonymous nobleman was moving as he expressed his opposition to the regent in these terms: 'Every time that the interest of he who governs a State is directly opposed to the State's interest, it follows that either the State must perish or the government must be changed.'[12]

In conclusion, the implications of the late sixteenth-century crisis and its subsequent seventeenth-century manifestations were also scrutinised by more profound minds which cut through the dense undergrowth of inherited concepts to trace back to its source the newly perceived stream of ideas. As a result of this exploration the intellectual map of Europe had to be redrawn along lines more familiar to our contemporary eye. The two great captains of this voyage of discovery were an Englishman, Thomas Hobbes, and a Dutchman, Baruch de Spinoza. Both recognised that, beyond the switch in emphasis from the ruler to the ruled and the subsequent debate over the nature and location of sovereignty, lay the ultimate reality of force, not itself a new factor but one which Hobbes and Spinoza incorporate with sophistication and bravura into their new cosmology.

Spinoza identifies the problem faced by sixteenth-century rulers whose power was increasingly bringing them towards the point of crisis: 'And, of course, those who believe that one man can hold the supreme right of a commonwealth by himself are greatly mistaken. For right is determined by power alone ... and the power of one man is far too small to bear so great a burden.'[13] He is not arguing here against the idea of monarchy but in favour of a notion of sovereignty which could support any form of government, a notion based on the perception of force as the only guarantor of the political order and on the absence of any rights prior to the sovereign's existence or outside the framework of his authority. In Hobbes' words: 'To this warre of every man against every man, this also is consequent; that nothing can be Unjust. The notions of Right and Wrong, Justice and Injustice have there no place. Where there is no common Power there is no Law: where no Law no Injustice.' Spinoza's vision of the state of nature is not dissimilar:

Anything, then, that an individual who is considered as subject only to nature judges to be useful to himself — either through the guidance of sound reason or through the impetus of passion — he has a perfect natural right to desire and indeed to appropriate by any means in his power — by force, fraud, entreaty, or however he finds it easiest; and hence a perfect natural right to regard as an enemy anyone who wishes to prevent him from satisfying his desire.[14]

To avoid the chaos implicit in such a situation, Spinoza provides for the establishment of a civil society held together by a sovereign possessing total power, of a kind not previously imagined, but necessary to offset the centrifugal nature of the warring factions over which he must govern, and to enforce and guarantee the division between subjects of rights and property. Such power is necessary too if the sovereign is to guarantee the subject against the pressures from without, for the end of sovereignty is 'the Peace of the Subjects within themselves, and their Defence against a common Enemy'.

Thus in the last resort, the sovereign is the arbiter of all. He is the arbiter of the law:

By private civil right we can only mean the individual's freedom to maintain himself in his own condition, a freedom defined by the edicts of the sovereign and upheld by its authority alone. . . . Wrong-doing occurs when one citizen or subject is forced by another to suffer some harm contrary to the civil law, or the edict of the sovereign. For wrong-doing can only be conceived in a political order; but no wrong can be done to their subjects by sovereigns, who have a right to do everything.[15]

Hobbes echoes Spinoza in emphasising that the sovereign is not subject to the civil law since he may change it at will if he finds it convenient so to do; nor is customary law observed for any other reason than that it meets with the sovereign's approval. The sovereign must be the final judge of right and wrong with the power to reward and punish; accordingly he must be able to levy taxes, raise troops, make war and peace as his view of the security and well-being of the people dictates. In pursuing these aims he must wield an awesome authority. For Spinoza, the power of sovereignty includes absolutely every means available to make men obey its commands, and, as for war, no other justification is needed than the will to wage it.[16]

Both authors also arrogated to the sovereign authority over three areas which had assumed significance in the course of the preceding decades: commerce, religion and property. Spinoza includes the regulation of commercial activities with such primary functions as the making of war and peace and the promulgation and repeal of laws, while Hobbes maintains the sovereign's right to assign the places and commodities in which the subject may traffic abroad; otherwise the lure of gain would lead men to export the means to harm the commonwealth to an enemy and to import commodities injurious to it. The sovereign should also decide how contracts between subjects should be made and validated. Both insisted upon the sovereign's authority over religion which exercised so powerful a hold over men's minds. It is not possible, so Hobbes maintained, to make a separate covenant with God, except through the sovereign's mediation. Spinoza asserted that 'it is also the function of the sovereign alone

to decide how everyone should practice piety towards his neighbour, that is, how everyone should obey God', and this function
included a controlling authority over moral judgments, the
appointment of pastors, the organisation and doctrine of the
church and provision for the poor. This view enables him to make
what may be considered as the clearest statement so far of the
new morality attached to the sometime amoral doctrine of reason
of state:

There is no doubt that devotion to country is the highest form of piety a man
can show; for once the state is destroyed nothing good can survive, but everything is put to hazard. . . . It follows that any act of piety towards a neighbour
would become an act of impiety if it caused harm to the state as a whole; while
any act of impiety towards him would be reckoned as piety if it were done for
the state's preservation.[17]

As a result of the crisis of princely authority a doctrine tentatively
propounded as a temporary, if necessary, alternative to the con-
ventional moral standards was itself in the process of becoming
the rule instead of the exception. When that process was complete
there would no longer be room for exceptions. Both, finally,
were adamant on the subject of ownership of property, which
they asserted belonged to the sovereign power.

Seeing therefore the Introduction of *Propriety* is an effect of Commonwealth,
[wrote Hobbes] which can do nothing but by the Person that Represents
it, it is the act only of the Soveraign; and consisteth in the Lawes, which none
can make that have not the Soveraign power. . . . In this Distribution, the First
Law, is for Division of the Land it selfe: wherein the Soveraign assigneth to
every man a portion, according as he, and not according as any Subject, or
any number of them, shall judge agreable to Equity, and the Common Good.

He expressed a similar view some nine years earlier in *De Cive*:

each particular citizen hath a propriety to which none of his fellow-citizens
hath right, because they are tied to the same laws; but he hath no propriety in
which the chief ruler (whose commands are the laws, whose will contains the
will of each man, and who, by every single person, is constituted the supreme
judge) hath not a right.[18]

Spinoza was of the same opinion: 'The fields and the whole
territory — and, if possible, the houses also — should be owned
by the state, that is by the sovereign.'[19]

The achievement of these two formidable intellects, therefore, was to offer a new image of political society, a society held together by force and utility with each member sacrificing his personal ambitions in the quest for a common sense of security. But there was little cohesion in such a union and the tendency of the various elements to fly apart made it necessary for the sovereign to wield unlimited and previously unimagined authority. The only justification for such power was that implied in the argument itself: reason of state was being revealed as the overriding justification and obligation of government. Anything was better than the chaos which would follow the breakdown or destruction of the political order. A once minor theme, quietly and diffidently introduced, was reaching an unexpected crescendo.

Not that the two men were entirely at one. Spinoza himself observed that 'With regard to politics the difference between Hobbes and me . . . consists in this, that I ever preserve the natural right intact so that the Supreme Power in a State has no more right over a subject than is proportionate to the power by which it is superior to the subject.'[20] It may be argued that Hobbes's view of the complete submission of self to a single common-will, with no reservation save that every member of the state should make a similar act of abnegation, leant further towards totalitarianism than Spinoza's. Yet the latter's tendency to equate the will of the king with the civil law and his person with the commonwealth, though expressed in the language of dynasticism, suggests that at the very least he was thinking along similar lines. Indeed Hobbes and Spinoza were united more than divided by their political ideas. Neither quite reached the concept of the impersonal state independent of ruler and ruled but both arrived at the very threshold of the idea.[21]

CONCLUSION

This enquiry was undertaken in the belief that no regular pattern was likely to emerge into which all the loose ends could readily be knitted and that such a theme by definition would defy neat chronological or phenomenological classification. So it has proved, though there are some tentative conclusions to be drawn and a pattern of sorts to be discerned. In essence we have traced the growth and after-effects of a general European crisis, brought about not by the emergence of power groups within the state but rather by the inflated authority of the prince against which these groups reacted. It is a mistake therefore to emphasize the role of the community or of its politically significant elements in this period at the expense of government pressure; still more misleading to dwell on the idea of community consciousness or proto-nationalism in an age when such a concept remained muted and elusive. The prince is the key figure upon whom attention should be focused. He it was whose very authority fed a growing appetite for power, who stood to benefit from the religious revolutions of the sixteenth century and, if not checked, from the rise of international commercial rivalry in the seventeenth. In any case, the prince's justification for his authority — *raison d'état* — was taken over by those governments which did successfully challenge him, for there was no discernable change, only an intensification in the crucial pressure which they had to face from without. Whether the threat was military, religious or economic, it remained true that external pressures rather than changes taking place in the domestic political, social or economic structure were decisive in the development of states, including the development of the modern state idea. That is not to argue that therefore this 'general crisis' was insignificant because whatever the outcome the new order had to face old problems. Rather is it to assert that the quest for sovereignty which was essentially what the crisis was about, revealed more clearly than ever before the real basis and extent of political power now being bequeathed by the prince to his successors. That power was handed on in different guises, some more elaborate than others, all seeking demurely to mask the reality which, as Hobbes remarked, men so little like to look upon.[1] In some states, those subject to what may be called the 'matryoshka syndrome' the true location of sovereignty remained elusive, in some others it was curbed for some time by the limitations of traditional restrictions, in others again it was unequivocally embodied in the person of the ruler. These differences may be accounted for simply in terms of historical accident, as the variety of local conditions, traditions and institutions shaped the course of the crisis though they could not forestall it. Equally, in the aftermath of the crisis its original stamp endured and it became clear that despite differences in emphasis there was a strong, converging tendency so that by the early eighteenth century the search for sovereignty was moving almost all the European countries towards the concept of the impersonal state.

In general it seems that moves in this direction had come more readily from states not solidly based upon a strong legal tradition, so that Russia stood at one end of the spectrum, Spain at the other. As in Spain, so in Germany too, the patrimonial ideal lingered on, countenanced by the Empire's dynastic character and by the fact that in many states the ruling family owned a high proportion of the land. In the emperor's Habsburg domains the strength of the proprietary tradition was further underlined by the manner in which different members of the dynasty had been called upon to preside over separate portions of the family inheritance; and not even the momentous acquisition of the whole of Hungary in the late seventeenth century brought any immediate sign of change in the family's concept of government. Yet there was in Germany one important exception. Prussia was a special case, for although it was one of the last states to make a move in that direction it was among the first in the eighteenth century to be identified as modern in the sense of this enquiry.[2]

The concept of the state as an abstract entity above and distinct from both government and governed, which has been the objective of our search, was coming to be understood in Europe before the end of the eighteenth century, when its alliance with the national idea produced a new dynamic force. Before this fusion had taken place, in the shadow of the Romantic movement, it was already possible to find more significance in Hobbes's words than most of his contemporaries could have done a century before; though they had not yet acquired the familiar, even ominous ring which they have for us: 'This is the Generation of that great LEVIATHAN, or rather (to speake more reverently) of that *Mortall God,* to which wee owe under the *Immortall God,* our peace and defence.'[3]

BIBLIOGRAPHICAL REFERENCES

Introduction

1. Herbert H. Rowen, 'Louis XIV and Absolutism', *Louis XIV and the Craft of Kingship*, Ed., John C. Rule, (Ohio 1969), p. 306.
2. J. A. Maravall, 'The Origins of the Modern State', *Journal of World History*, VI 4 (1961), p. 795.

Chapter 1. *The rise of the princes*

1. J. Burckhardt, *The Civilisation of the Renaissance in Italy* (Mentor ed., New York 1961), p. 77.
2. R. Pipes (Ed.), *Karamzin's Memoir on Ancient and Modern Russia* (Cambridge, Mass. 1959), pp. 140–1.
3. B. Dmytryshyn (Ed.), *Medieval Russia: a Source Book, 900–1700* (New York 1967), p. 153.
4. ibid., p. 157.
5. Sigmund von Herberstein, *Description of Moscow and Muscovy*, Ed., B. Picard (London 1969), pp. 61–2.
6. Anthony Cross (Ed.), *Russia under Western Eyes, 1517–1825* (London 1971), p. 62.
7. ibid. p. 63.
8. ibid. p. 64.
9. Olivier de la Marche, *Mémoires*, Ed., J. F. Michaud and J. J. F. Poujoulat (Paris 1837), p. 580; Antoinette Huon, 'Le Thème du Prince dans les Entrées parisiennes au XVIᵉ Siècle', *Les Fêtes de la Renaissance*, Ed., J. Jacquot (Paris 1956), p. 22.

10. Olivier de la Marche, op. cit., p. 534.

11. B. Castiglione, *The Book of the Courtier* (Everyman ed., London 1928), p. 73.

12. ibid., p. 68; see also Pauline M. Smith, *The Anti-Courtier Trend in Sixteenth Century French Literature* (Geneva 1966), p. 60.

13. Castiglione, op. cit., pp. 290-1.

14. G. Budé, *L'Institution du Prince* (in *Le Prince dans la France des XVIe et XVIIe siècles*), Eds., C. Bontems, L.-P Raybaud, J.-P. Brancourt (Paris 1965), pp. 79 & 84.

15. Huon, op. cit., p. 26.

16. Sir Thomas Malory, *Morte d' Arthur*, Everyman ed., 2 vols. (London 1908), ii, 400; see also, for example, E. Hall, *Chronicle* (London 1809), pp. 584-6; *Calendar of Letters and Papers, Foreign and Domestic, of the Reign of Henry VIII, 1509-47*, Eds., J. S. Brewer, J. Gairdner and R. H. Brodie, 21 vols. (London 1862-1910), i, 380.

17. *The Epistles of Erasmus*, Ed., F. M. Nichols, 3 vols. (London 1918), iii, 345 & 361.

18. Sir Thomas Smith, *De Republica Anglorum*, Ed., L. Alston (Cambridge 1906), pp. 62-3.

19. C. C. Willard, 'The Concept of True Nobility at the Burgundian Court', *Studies in the Renaissance*, XIV (1967), pp. 35 & 45.

20. Burckhardt, op. sit., p. 65; C. H. Clough, 'The Relations Between the English and Urbino Courts, 1474-1508', *Studies in the Renaissance*, XIV (1967), pp. 202 et seq.

21. Burckhardt, op. cit., p. 176; F. Schevill, *The Medici* (London 1950), pp. 163-8; E. H. Gombrich, 'The Early Medici as Patrons of Art: A Survey of Primary Sources', *Italian Renaissance Studies*, Ed., E. F. Jacob (London 1960), pp. 310-11.

22. H. J. Cohn, 'The Early Renaissance Court in Heidelberg', *European Studies Review*, i, 4 (1971), p. 322.

23. K. F. Lewalski, 'Sigismund I of Poland: Renaissance King and Patron', *Studies in the Renaissance*, XIV (1967), pp. 49-72; C. A. Macartney, *Hungary. A Short History* (Edinburgh 1962), pp. 54-6.

24. Huon, op. cit., p. 27.

25. Herberstein, op. cit, p. 62.

26. ibid., p. 43.

27. Philippe de Commynes, *Mémoires*, Ed., J. Calmette, 3 vols. (Paris 1925), ii, 227.

28. Claude de Seyssel, *La Monarchie de France*, Ed., J. Poujol (Paris, 1961), p. 116.

29. D. Erasmus, *Enchiridion Militis Christiani*, Ed., R. Himelick (Indiana 1963), p. 153.

30. Castiglione, op. cit. p. 277.

31. *Epistles*, op. cit., iii, 46.

32. R. C. Howes, *The Testaments of the Grand Princes of Moscow* (Cornell 1967), pp. 268–9.

33. J. L. I. Fennell, *The Correspondence between Prince A. M. Kurbsky and Tsar Ivan IV of Russia, 1564–1579* (Cambridge 1955), p. 105. However, it should also be noted that the genuineness of this correspondence has recently been challenged by Edward L. Keenan, *The Kurbskii-Groznyi Apocrypha. The Seventeenth-Century Genesis of the "Correspondence" Attributed to Prince A. M. Kurbskii and Tsar Ivan IV* (Cambridge, Mass. 1971). There is an extensive literature on the subject of the Third Rome, including N. Chayev, 'Moskva Tretii Rim v Politicheskoy Praktikye Moskovskogo Pravitelstva XVI Veka' (Moscow the Third Rome in the Political Practice of 16th century Muscovite Government), *Istoricheskiye Zapiski* (1945), pp. 3–23; D. Stremukhov, 'Moscow the Third Rome', *Speculum*, XXVIII (1953), pp. 84–101; A. V. Solovyev, *Holy Russia: the History of a Religious-Social Idea* (The Hague 1959).

34. Fennell, op cit., p. 125.

35. ibid., pp. 189 & 195.

36. J. L. I. Fennell, *Ivan the Great of Moscow* (London 1963), pp. 212–16.

37. D. Erasmus, *In Praise of Folly*, Sesame Library ed. (London 1951), p. 173; Lewalski, op. cit., pp. 58–9; Budé, op. cit., p. 112.

38. J. G. Gaztambide, 'The Holy See and the Reconquest of the Kingdom of Granada (1479–1492)', *Spain in the Fifteenth Century, 1564–1579*, Ed. R. Highfield (London 1972), p. 370.

39. N. Machiavelli, *The Prince*, Everyman ed. (London 1958), pp. 7–8.

40. *Instruction de l'Empereur Charles V à Philippe II son Fils* (The Hague 1788), p. 6.

41. Machiavelli: op. cit., pp. 109–10; *The Discourses on the First Ten Books of Titus Livius*, Modern Library ed. (New York 1950), p. 182.

42. D. M. Bueno de Mesquita, 'Ludovico Sforza and his Vassals', P. J. Jones, 'The End of Malatesta Rule in Rimini', *Italian Renaissance Studies,* op. cit., pp. 205 & 223; P. Laven, *Renaissance Italy, 1464–1534* (London 1966), pp. 137–8.

43. A. von Martin, *Sociology of the Renaissance* (London 1944), pp. 71–2.

44. S. Anglo, *Spectacle, Pageantry and Early Tudor Policy* (Oxford 1969), pp. 46–7; Polydore Vergil, *Anglica Historia*, Ed., D. Hay, Camden Series, LXXIV (London 1950), p. XXXIV; C. J. Armstrong, 'An Italian Astrologer at the Court of Henry VII', *Italian Renaissance Studies,* op. cit., p. 450.

45. M. Cherniavsky, *Tsar and People. Studies in Russian Myths* (Yale 1961), p. 41; Macartney, op. cit., p. 55.

Chapter 2.   The limits and implications of princely authority

1. F. Gilbert, *Machiavelli and Guicciardini* (Princeton 1965), p. 177; J. H. Hexter, 'Il Principe and lo Stato', *Studies in the Renaissance,* IV (1957), p. 118. For a recent discussion of an associated theme, see N. Rubinstein, 'Notes on the word *stato* in Florence before Machiavelli', *Florilegium Historiale: Essays presented to Wallace K. Ferguson,* Eds., J. G. Rowe and W. H. Stockdale (Toronto 1971), pp. 319–20.

2. Dmytryshyn, *Medieval Russia,* p. 153; Howes, *The Testaments,* p. 269.

3. Budé, *L'Institution du Prince,* pp. 81–2.

4. Bodleian Library, Oxford, MS. Rawl. C.293: 'A Relation and Instruction concerning the State of Milan', by Don Scipio di Castro [hereafter Castro], fol. 35v; *Instruction de l'Empereur Charles V,* pp. 8–9.

5. C. H. McIlwain (Ed.), *The Political Works of James I* (Cambridge 1918), *Basilikon Doron. Or His Majesty's Instructions to his Dearest Son, Henry the Prince,* p. 18; *The Trew Law of Free Monarchies,* p. 55.

6. McIlwain, *The Political Works, The Trew Law of Free Monarchies,* p. 55.

7. Seyssel, *La Monarchie de France,* pp. 150 & 157; *Instruction de l'Empereur Charles V,* p. 28.

8. F. Guicciardini, *Maxims and Reflections of a Renaissance Statesman* [Ricordi] (New York 1965), p. 69.

9. Thomas More, *Utopia* (Penguin ed., London 1965), p. 62; Machiavelli, *The Prince,* p. 101.

10. Machiavelli: *The Discourses,* pp. 164, 261 & 402; *The Prince,* pp. 22, 105.

11. J. de Mariana, *The General History of Spain* (London 1699), p. 458.

12. Erasmus, *Enchiridion,* p. 65.

13. Budé, op. cit., pp. 49, 60, 91 & 103; Castro, op. cit., fols. 35v et seq.

14. Castiglione, *The Book of the Courtier,* p. 277.

15. Budé, op. cit., p. 138.

16. See the editor's remarks in his preface to Budé, p. 54.

17. Castro, op. cit., fol. 28.

18. Machiavelli, *The Discourses,* p. 439; *Instruction de l'Empereur Charles V,* p. 39.

19. Seyssel, op. cit., p. 104; Erasmus, *Enchiridion,* p. 65; Guicciardini, *Maxims,* p. 125.

20. Machiavelli, *The Prince,* pp. 54 & 122; *Instruction de l'Empereur Charles V,* p. 12.

21. Commynes, *Mémoires*, ii, 217–18.

22. F. Guicciardini, *The History of Florence* (London 1966), pp. 9–10.

23. *Instruction de l'Empereur Charles V*, pp. 12–19; the details of Isabella d'Este's letter to Ludovico Sforza may be found in Laven, *Renaissance Italy*, p. 147.

24. Guicciardini, *Maxims*, p. 64.

25. D. Hay, *The Italian Renaissance in its Historical Background* (Cambridge 1961), p. 139.

26. F. Guicciardini, *The History of Italy*, Ed., H. R. Trevor-Roper (London 1966), pp. 86–7; A. Vagts, 'The Balance of Power: Growth of an Idea', *World Politics*, i (1948), p. 97.

27. Machiavelli: *The Prince*, pp. 65 & 79; *The Discourses*, p. 503.

28. C. Grayson (Ed.), *Francesco Guicciardini: Selected Writings* (Oxford 1965), *Considerations on the 'Discourses' of Machiavelli*, p. 62.

29. Castiglione, op. cit., p. 281.

30. In his *Anti-Machiavel Studies on Voltaire and the Eighteenth Century*, V, Ed., T. Bestermann (Geneva 1958), p. 229.

31. G. Mattingly, *Renaissance Diplomacy* (London 1965), pp. 140 & 152; Guicciardini, *Maxims*, p. 40.

32. Seyssel, op. cit., pp. 190–1.

33. *Instruction de l'Empereur Charles V*, pp. 43-5, 67; H. G. Koenigsberger, 'The Statecraft of Philip II', *European Studies Review*, i, I (1971), pp. 10–11.

34. Sir Thomas Smith, *De Republica Anglorum*, p. 63; R. Hooker, *Of the Laws of Ecclesiastical Polity*, Everyman ed., 2 vols. (London 1907), i, 199; McIlwain, *The Political Works*, p. 55.

35. Machiavelli: *The Discourses*, pp. 108, 124 & 208; *The Prince*, pp. 99–100. Compare the comments of A. P. d'Entrèves, *The Notion of the State* (Oxford 1967), pp. 37–8.

36. Guicciardini, *Maxims*, p. 119.

37. Erasmus, *In Praise of Folly*, p. 174; More, op. cit., p. 42; Seyssel, op. cit., p. 191.

38. Castro, op. cit., fol. 41r.

39. More, op. cit., p. 108.

40. Erasmus, *In Praise of Folly*, pp. 75 & 161–2.

41. *Instruction de l'Empereur Charles V*, pp. 7, 20, 36, 44–5 & 73–80.

42. Guicciardini: *The History of Florence*, pp. 9–10; *Maxims*, pp. 77 & 84.

43. Erasmus, *Enchiridion Militis Christiani*, pp. 152–54.

44. Erasmus, *In Praise of Folly*, p. 159.

45. *Instruction de l'Empereur Charles V*, p. 2.

46. Seyssel, op cit., pp. 219–21.

47. More, op. cit., p. 128.

48. Maravall, 'The Origins of the Modern State', p. 797.

49. J. H. Elliott, 'Revolution and Continuity in Early Modern Europe', *Past and Present*, XLII (1969), p. 49.

50. R. M. Pidal. 'The Catholic Kings according to Machiavelli and Castiglione', *Spain in the Fifteenth Century, 1369–1516*, Ed., R. Highfield (London 1972), p. 412.

51. F. L. Baumer, 'England, the Turk and the Common Corps of Christendom', *American Historical Review*, L, 1 (1944), p. 34, note 49; Baumer, 'The Conception of Christendom in Renaissance England', *Journal of the History of Ideas*, VI, 2 (1945), p. 142.

52. Maravall, op. cit., p. 806. Isabella's will is printed in full in M. B. Gaibrois, *Isabel de Castilla, Reina Catolica de España* (Madrid 1964), pp. 235–71, the clause relating to foreigners on pp. 248–9.

53. P. Geyl, *The Revolt of the Netherlands, 1559–1609* (London 1958), p. 102; even Philip II eventually acknowledged the need to employ native troops in the Netherlands' struggle rather than Spaniards or Italians, *Correspondance de Philippe II sur les Affaires des Pays-Bas*, 4 vols. (Brussels 1940–60), i, 39–41 & 49.

54. McIlwain, *The Political Works, Basilikon Doron*, p. 32.

55. Machiavelli, *The Prince*, p. 76.

56. Seyssel, *La Monarchie de France*, pp. 170–1.

57. Maravall, 'The Origins of the Modern State', p. 808.

Chapter 3.   The reality of power

1. J. H. Shennan, *Government and Society in France, 1461–1661* (London 1969), p. 79.

2. J. Russell Major, *Representative Institutions in Renaissance France, 1421–1559* (Wisconsin 1960), pp. 6–7, chooses to represent both these developments as manifestations of decentralisation. Though on one level they clearly were, his overriding emphasis on the decentralising nature of French Renaissance monarchy is open to challenge. Compare R. J. Knecht, *Francis I and Absolute Monarchy* (London 1969), pp. 23–7.

3. J. H. Shennan, *The Parlement of Paris* (London 1968), pp. 78–82.

4. ibid., pp. 178 et seq., 193–7.

5. R. J. Knecht, 'The Concordat of 1516: a Reassessment', *Government in Reformation Europe, 1520–1560*, Ed., H. J. Cohn (London 1971), pp. 109–10.

6. ibid., Knecht, pp. 97 & 109.

7. Compare the remarks of F. Meinecke, *Machiavellism. The Doctrine of Raison d'Etat and its Place in Modern History* (London 1962), pp. 9–10.

8. The most detailed and complete account of these developments is to be found in R. Doucet, *Les Institutions de la France au XVIe siècle*, 2 vols. (Paris 1948); they are more briefly summarised in Shennan, *Government and Society* pp. 13–60.

9. R. Doucet, *Etude sur le Gouvernement de François Ier dans ses Rapports avec le Parlement de Paris*, 2 vols. (Paris 1921–6), i, 60–3.

10. R. M. Pidal, 'The Significance of the Reign of Isabella the Catholic, According to Her Contemporaries', *Spain in the Fifteenth Century, 1369–1516*, Ed., R. Highfield (London 1972), p. 381.

11. J. B. Perez, 'The Science of Law in the Spain of the Catholic Kings', *Spain in the Fifteenth Century, 1369–1516*, Ed., R. Highfield (London 1972), p. 280.

12. G. Lewy, *Constitutionalism and Statecraft during the Golden Age of Spain* (Geneva 1960), p. 58.

13. J. H. Elliott, *Imperial Spain, 1469–1716* (London 1963), p. 65.

14. R. M. Pidal, 'The Catholic King's, p. 412.

15. J. Vicens Vives, 'The Administrative Structure of the State in the Sixteenth and Seventeenth Centuries', *Government in Reformation Europe, 1520–1560*, Ed., H. J. Cohn (London 1971), p. 68.

16. A. W. Lovett, 'A New Governor for the Netherlands: the Appointment of Don Luis de Requesens, Comendador Mayor de Castilla', *European Studies Review*, i, 2 (1971), p. 97.

17. J. A. Maravell, *La Philosophie Politique Espagnole au XVIIe Sièle dans ses Rapports avec l'Esprit de la Contre-Réforme* (Paris 1955), p. 241.

18. Like many historians I use the term 'bureaucracy' to denote a degree of administrative complexity rather than the systematically defined socio-logical phenomenon elaborated for example by Max Weber, *Economy and Society*, 3 vols. (New York 1968) vol. 3, pp. 956–8 and S. N. Eisenstadt, *The Political Systems of Empires* (New York 1963), pp. 21–2. In this matter I am much indebted to my colleague at Lancaster, Dr. C. H. Church, who has allowed me to use his, as yet unpublished, work on the growth of the French bureaucracy. In the key second chapter of that work he demon-strates the variety of definitions which have been given to the word, and castigates the historian in particular for his failure to make an effective contribution. His own definition, based upon the conclusions of some thirty scholars, leads me to believe that, in the technical sense at least, 'bureaucracy' does not exist in the period covered by this volume for, to put it briefly, the administration at no time possesses a life of its own. However, it seems to me that the non-technical definition offered above still has meaning and validity in terms of the age under review.

19. R. E. Giesey, *If Not, Not. The Oath of the Aragonese and the Legendary Laws of Sorbrarbe* (Princeton 1968), p. 6.

20. J. H. Elliott, *The Revolt of the Catalans* (Cambridge 1963), p. 547.

21. See above, p. 25.

22. J. Blum, *Lord and Peasant in Russia from the Ninth to the Nineteenth Century,* Atheneum ed. (New York 1964), p. 234.

23. J. L. H. Keep, 'The Decline of the Zemsky Sobor', *Slavonic and East European Review,* XXXVI (1957), pp. 100–22.

24. Cherniavsky, *Tsar and People,* pp. 87–8.

25. by O. Hoetzsch, *The Evolution of Russia* (London 1966), p. 44.

26. V. O. Kliuchevsky, *A Course in Russian History: the Seventeenth Century,* vol. III of the justly celebrated *Kurs Russkoi Istorii,* trans., Chicago 1968), pp. 70–1.

27. *L'Anti-Machiavel,* p. 175.

28. G. R. Elton, *The Tudor Revolution in Government* (Cambridge 1962), p. 423.

29. G. E. Aylmer, *The King's Servants* (London 1961), p. 464.

30. W. G. Zeefeld, *Foundations of Tudor Policy* (Harvard 1948), p. 155; see also the interesting article by C. H. McIlwain, 'The English Common Law, Barrier against Absolutism', *American Historical Review,* XLIX, I (1943), pp. 28–9.

31. Machiavelli, *The Prince,* p. 93.

32. M. Roberts, *The Early Vasas* (Cambridge 1968), p. 117.

33. ibid., p. 44.

34. E. H. Dunkley, *The Reformation in Denmark* (London 1948), pp. 74–6.

35. See G. R. Elton, 'An Early Tudor Poor Law', *Economic History Review,* 2nd Series, VI, I (1953), *passim.*

36. The standard edition of Peter's important Ecclesiastical Regulation is in vol. 2 of P. V. Verkhovskoi, *Uchrezhdenie Dukhovnoi Kollegii i Dukhovnyi Reglament* (The Establishment of the Ecclesiastical College and the Ecclesiastical Regulation), 2 vols. (Rostov-on-Don 1916). See the remarks of J. Cracraft, *The Church Reform of Peter the Great* (London 1971), pp. ix–x.

37. V. O. Klyuchevsky, *Peter the Great* (London 1965), p.259 ; Cherniavsky, op cit., pp. 82–3; M. Raeff, *Origins of the Russian Intelligentsia* (New York 1966), pp. 34–70. The best-known example of Peter's own expressed opinion is to be found in his address to the Russian troops before Pultava, *Pis' ma i Bumagi Petra Velikogo* (Letters and Despatches of Peter the Great), 9 vols. (Moscow 1912–64), IX, I, p. 226. The contrast between taking up arms for Peter and for the state (ne . . . za Petra, no za gosudarstvo') is underlined both by Peter's insistence that his life is of no importance com-

pared with the survival of Russia and by the use of the word 'gosudarstvo' with its still highly personalised connotation (*gosudar'*, prince or lord) in contradistinction to the ruler's own person. For a full translation of this order, see *A Source Book for Russian History from Early Times to 1917*, Eds., G. Vernadsky *et al.*, 3 vols. (Yale 1972), ii, 365.

38. A point recently made by Cracraft, op. cit., p. viii. The same matter is also discussed by W. K. Medlin and C. G. Patrinelis, *Renaissance Influences and Religious Reforms in Russia* (Geneva 1971), *passim*.

39. C. H. Wilson, *The Dutch Republic* (London 1968), p. 18.

40. H. Bornkamm, *Luther's World of Thought* (Missouri 1958), pp. 241-3; K. Holl, *The Cultural Significance of the Reformation*, trans. (New York 1959), pp. 52-3.

41. B. Pullan, *Rich and Poor in Renaissance Venice* (Oxford 1971), p. 638. The same author's 'Service to the Venetian State: aspects of myth and reality in the early seventeenth century', *Studi Secenteschi*, V (1964), pp. 95–147, and 'The Occupations and Investments of the Venetian Nobility in the Middle and Late Sixteenth Century', to be published shortly in *Venetian Studies* (Ed. J. R. Hale), inquire into the continuing success of the ruling aristocratic class in this surviving enclave of Republicanism, in identifying its interests with those of the state. (I am indebted to Professor Pullan for providing me with an off-print of the first of these articles and the typescript, before publication, of the second.)

42. Olwen Hufton, 'Begging, Vagrancy, Vagabondage and the Law: an Aspect of the Problem of Poverty in Eighteenth-century France', *European Studies Review*, ii, **2** (1972), p. 97; Elliott, *Imperial Spain*, p. 181.

43. Holl, op. cit., pp. 170–1.

44. Compare the sixteenth century comments of A. Gentili, *De Iure Belli Libris Tres*, 2 vols. (Oxford 1933), ii, 56–9.

Chapter 4.   *The quest for sovereignty* (*I*):
Revolts in France and the Low Countries

1. Shennan, *Government and Society*, pp. 39–41 & 61.

2. H. G. Koenigsberger, 'Western Europe and the Power of Spain', *New Cambridge Modern History*, vol. III (Cambridge 1968), p. 281, reprinted in *The Habsburgs and Europe, 1516–1660* (London 1971); H. G. Koenigsberger and G. L. Mosse, *Europe in the Sixteenth Century* (London 1968), p. 40.

3. The *Vindiciae* has been published in a seventeenth-century English translation by H. J. Laski, *A Defence of Liberty against Tyrants* (London 1924): see

particularly pp. 104–9, 143, 165 & 199; J. W. Allen, *A History of Political Thought in the Sixteenth Century* (London 1960), pp. 314–31.

4. ibid., pp. 383–5.

5. Compare, for example, his conflicting remarks on the sovereign prince's freedom from prosecution by his subjects (pp. 67 & 127), on the harshness of the prince's image (pp. 64 & 138), on the subjects' rights in matters of taxation (pp. 32 & 189), J. Bodin, *Six Books of the Commonwealth*, Ed., M. J. Tooley (Oxford 1955).

6. ibid., p. 186.

7. ibid., pp. 20–1.

8. ibid., p. 19.

9. ibid., pp. 134, 141 & 158–9.

10. ibid., p. 35.

11. ibid., p. 188.

12. See the important article by H. G. Koenigsberger, 'The Organisation of Revolutionary Parties in France and the Netherlands during the Sixteenth Century', *Journal of Modern History*, XXVII (1955), pp. 335–51.

13. J. Meuvret, 'Comment les Français du XVIIᵉ siècle voyaient l'Impôt', *Comment les Français voyaient la France au XVIIᵉ siècle,* Ed., R. Mousnier (Paris 1955), pp. 59–78; M. Marion, *Les Impôts Directs sous l'Ancien Régime* (Paris 1910), pp. 242–3, 270.

14. Koenigsberger, *The Habsburgs and Europe*, p. 19.

15. H. H. Rowen (Ed.), *The Low Countries in Early Modern Times* (New York 1972), pp. 27–8.

16. This indecisiveness is well illustrated in two articles by A. W. Lovett, 'A New Governor for the Netherlands', pp. 95 et seq., and 'The Governorship of Don Luis de Requesens, 1573–76. A Spanish View', *European Studies Review,* ii, 3 (1972), p. 191.

17. Geyl, *The Revolt of the Netherlands,* p. 102.

18. Koenigsberger, 'The Statecraft of Philip II', p. 12.

19 Lovett, 'A New Governor for the Netherlands', pp 89–90 & 103.

20. Rowen, *The Low Countries in Early Modern Times,* pp. 44–5.

21. ibid., p. 72–3.

22. ibid., pp. 93 & 102.

23. K. H. D. Haley, *The Dutch in the Seventeenth Century* (London 1972), p. 71.

24. Wilson, *The Dutch Republic,* p. 176.

25. R. Mousnier, *Les XVIᵉ et XVIIᵉ siècles* (Paris 1961), p. 261.

26. See, for example, the article by H. H. Rowen, 'The Revolution that wasn't: the coup d'état of 1650 in Holland'', *European Studies Review,* iv, 2 (1974).

Chapter 5.   The quest for sovereignty (II):
Commercial rivalry and the English experience

1. On Laffemas, see the article by G. Mongrédien, 'Isaac de Laffemas, d'après des Documents Inédits', *Revue des Questions Historiques*, CVII–CVIII (1928), pp. 9–10; on Gustav Vasa, E. Heckscher, *An Economic History of Sweden* (Harvard 1954), p. 61; on Anika Stroganov, Y. Semyonov, *Siberia* (London 1963), pp. 25–39.

2. P. S. Lewis, *Later Medieval France, The Polity* (London 1968), p. 54.

3. *Calendar of Letters and State Papers relating to English Affairs, preserved principally in the Archives of Simancas*, vol. I: Elizabeth, 1558–1567, Ed., M. A. S. Hume, 4 vols. (London 1892–9), p. 572.

4. T. W. Fulton, *The Sovereignty of the Sea* (London 1911), p. 148.

5. G. N. Clark and W. J. M. van Eysinga, *The Colonial Conferences between England and the Netherlands in 1613 and 1615*, 2 vols. (Leyden 1940 & 1951), ii, 143.

6. Fulton, op. cit., p. 136.

7. McIlwain, *The Political Works. Speech of 21 March, 1609*, pp. 323–4; R. W. K. Hinton, *The Eastland Trade and the Common Weal in the Seventeenth Century* (Cambridge 1959), p. 60; J. Viner, 'Power versus Plenty as Objectives of Foreign Policy in the Seventeenth and Eighteenth Centuries', *World Politics*, i (1948), p. 18.

8. McIlwain, *The Political Works. A Remonstrance for the Right of Kings, and the Independance of their Crownes*, pp. 265–6.

9. Fulton, op. cit., p. 257; see also the comments of J. R. Jones, 'English Attitudes to Europe in the Seventeenth Century', *Britain and the Netherlands in Europe and Asia*, Eds., J. S. Bromley and E. H. Kossmann (London 1968), pp. 42–3.

10. Thomas Mun, *England's Treasure by Forraign Trade* (Oxford 1928), pp. 52 & 88.

11. L. A. Harper, *The English Navigation Laws* (Columbia 1939), p. 39; J. R. Jones, *Britain and Europe in the Seventeenth Century* (London 1966), p. 47.

12. Hinton, op. cit., p. 53.

13. ibid., p. 154.

14. J. W. Smit, 'The Netherlands and Europe in the Seventeenth and Eighteenth Centuries', *Britain and the Netherlands in Europe and Asia*, p. 26; P. de la Court, *The True Interest and Political Maxims of the Republic of Holland and West-Friesland* (London 1702), pp. 376–7; see also the very similar comments of J. Child, *Brief Observations concerning Trade and Interest of Money* (London 1668), p. 3.

15. Sir William Temple, *Observations upon the United Provinces of the Netherlands* (Cambridge 1932), p. 81.

16. Jones, *Britain and Europe in the Seventeenth Century*, p. 97; V. Barbour, *Capitalism in Amsterdam in the Seventeenth Century* (Michigan 1963), pp. 40 & 131.

17. A. de Montchrétien, *Traicté de l'Oeconomie Politique* (Paris 1615): *Collection des Economistes et des Réformateurs Sociaux de la France*, introduced by T. Funck-Brentano (Paris 1889), p. 248; A. D. Lublinskaya, *French Absolutism: the Crucial Phase, 1620–9* (Cambridge 1968), p. 137.

18. Rowen, *The Low Countries in Early Modern Times*, pp. 161–2.

19. The subject is discussed by Margaret Priestley, 'Anglo-French Trade and the 'Unfavourable Balance' Controversy, 1660–1685', *Economic History Review*, 2nd Series, IV, 1 (1951), pp. 37–52; see also the important work by L. Rothkrug, *Opposition to Louis XIV* (Princeton 1965), especially pp. 435 et seq., for a discussion of mercantilist theory towards the end of Louis' reign.

20. The background to international rivalry in the Baltic may be studied in W. Kirchner, *The Rise of the Baltic Question* (Delaware 1954). See also L. V. Cherepnin, 'Some problems of trade in the Baltic between Russia and the countries of Western Europe in the 17th century in Soviet historiography', *Anglo-Soviet Conference of Historians* (London 1963), pp. 9–11.

21. J. B. Wolf, *Louis XIV*, Panther ed. (London 1970), pp. 205–6; M. Malowist, 'Les Mouvements d'Expansion en Europe aux XVe et XVIe siècles', *Annales, Economies, Sociétés, Civilisations*, 17th year, 5 (1962), p. 927.

22. H. Grotius, *The Law of War and Peace* (New York 1925), p.138 ; see also V. E. Hrabar (Ed.), *De Legatis et Legationibus* (Dorpat 1905), which prints 15 such treatises dating from the sixteenth century and 25 from the seventeenth, and E. Nys, *Les Origines du Droit International* (Brussels 1894), *passim*.

23. Grotius, op. cit., pp. 102–3.

24. ibid., pp. 111, 314, 385, 796–7 & 807.

25. McIlwain, *The Political Works, Basilikon Doron*, p. 42; J. P. Kenyon, *The Stuart Constitution* (Cambridge 1966), p. 84.

26 E. H. Kantorowicz, *The King's Two Bodies* (Princeton 1957), pp. 7 & 21–3.

27. McIlwain, *The Political Works, Speech to Parliament on 19 March, 1603*, p. 272.

Chapter 6.   Towards the Leviathan

1. J. H. Elliott, 'The Statecraft of Olivares', *The Diversity of History: Essays in Honour of Sir Herbert Butterfield*, Eds., J. H. Elliott and H. G. Koenigsberger (London 1970), pp. 129–32.

2. Cardinal de Richelieu, *Testament Politique*, Ed., L. André (Paris 1947), pp. 128 & 276.

3. ibid., pp. 343-4, 380. This volume was completed before the appearance in England of an important work on Richelieu by William F. Church, *Richelieu and Reason of State* (Princeton 1972). The author's wide-ranging analysis cannot be encapsulated in a footnote but his overall conclusion, tending to confirm the transitional nature of the cardinal's thought, may be cited: 'Richelieu and his spokesmen . . . genuinely believed that they had adumbrated a scheme of Christian politics which, in the hands of a devout king and minister, justified all measures that they might deem necessary to strengthen the Christian state. . . . It remained for others after him to develop the concept of reason of state of the modern world' (p. 513).

4. Louis XIV, *Mémoires for the Instruction of the Dauphin*, Ed., P. Sonnino (New York 1970), p. 77.

5. ibid., pp. 64, 68.

6. ibid., p. 165.

7. Wolf, *Louis XIV*, p. 763.

8. P. Grimblot (Ed.), *Letters of William III and Louis XIV and of their Ministers*, 2 vols. (London 1848), ii, 280-1.

9. H. M. A. Keens-Soper, 'The French Political Academy, 1712: The School for Ambassadors', *European Studies Review*, ii, 4 (1972), p. 334.

10. Maravall, *La Philosophie Politique Espagnole*, p. 164. C. H. Church remarks in his typescript, op. cit., ch. 2, p. 67 that 'One has in the final instance to accept that different social and historical situations will have differing, and probably contradictory, outcomes in terms of administrative history.'

11. Bibliothèque de l'Arsenal, Paris, MS. 3857, *Recueil de Mémoires sur la Régence du duc d'Orléans*, p. 115; Bibliothèque Nationale, Paris, *Collection Clairambault*, 529, *Mémoires et Documents concernant la Régence du duc d'Orléans (1715-23) et les finances jusqu'en 1738*, p. 293.

12. Archives du Ministère des Affaires Etrangères, Paris, *Mémoires et Documents, France*, 311, f.97^r; 445, ff.177^v-178^r.

13. B. de Spinoza, *The Political Works*, Ed., A. G. Wernham (Oxford 1958). *Tractatus Politicus*, p. 317.

14. T. Hobbes, *Leviathan*, Everyman ed. (London 1949), p. 66; Spinoza, *Tractatus Theologico-Politicus*, p. 127.

15. Hobbes, *Leviathan*, p. 144.

16. Spinoza, *Tractatus Theologico-Politicus*, p. 151; *Tractatus Politicus*, p. 295.

17. Spinoza, *Tractatus Theologico-Politicus*, pp. 211 & 213.

18. Hobbes, *Leviathan*, p. 131; *De Cive* (New York 1949), p. 80.

19. Spinoza, *Tractatus Politicus*, p. 321.

20. B. de Spinoza, *The Correspondence*, Ed., A. Wolf (London 1966), p. 269.

21. The same may be said of other distinguished seventeenth-century com-
    mentators. See, for example: S. Pufendorf, *Of the Law of Nature and
    Nations* (London 1729), p. 646; *The Political Writings of Leibniz*, Ed.,
    P. Riley (Cambridge 1972), *Caesarinus Fürstenerius* (1677), p. 117. Locke,
    on the other hand, seems still firmly wedded to the idea that governor and
    governed together constitute the political body: J. Locke, *Two Treatises of
    Government*, Ed., P. Laslett (Cambridge 1967), p. 228.

                                    Conclusion

 1. Hobbes, *De Cive*, p. 83.

 2. F. Hertz, *The Development of the German Public Mind* (London 1962), pp. 24
    & 68; L. Krieger, *The German Idea of Freedom* (Boston 1957), pp. 22–6.

 3. Hobbes, *Leviathan*, p. 89. See also F. Chabod, *L'Idea di Nazione* (Bari 1967),
    p. 17.

INDEX

INDEX